MOSAIC
History and Technique

MOSAIC
History and Technique

Peter Fischer

16 color plates
104 monochrome plates
16 line illustrations

McGRAW-HILL BOOK COMPANY
New York · Toronto

CORNELIÆ FILIÆ

INSPIRANDÆ

GRATUS AUCTOR

Rewritten and revised by the author from his book
Das Mosaik, originally published in German

© 1971 Thames and Hudson Ltd, London
© 1969 Anton Schroll & Co, Vienna and Munich

Plates printed in Italy

Text printed in Switzerland

Bound in Germany

ISBN 07-021078-0

Library of Congress Catalog Card Number: 74-148984

Contents

Introduction: The Meaning of Mosaic

Mosaic is both a queen and a Cinderella among the arts; other arts may be greater, but none can be finer. Yet it is often classed as merely a craft and literally trodden underfoot. Hardly anyone can name a single artist in this field, or remember when he last saw a mosaic, although he may have passed one only the day before. The all-devouring art and antiques trade will rarely touch these unwieldy panels of coloured bits and pieces. Publishers have been busy erecting impressive armchair museums of world art, but, since the books by Adrien Blanchet, Edgar Waterman Anthony and Josef Ludwig Fischer (all published in the twenties and thirties, and long out of print and out of date), there has been no comprehensive account of the art of mosaic throughout its history.

There are, of course, plenty of scholarly analyses and magnificent picture volumes devoted to the mosaics of individual places such as Pompeii and Ravenna, or spanning particular periods, such as the Byzantine era, and their authors' painstaking researches have provided the indispensable basis for the broad survey attempted here. If such a survey has not been undertaken before, it may be because specialists are kept busy enough by the constant growth of new material on their own particular plots of this vast field. For instance, it was not until 1963 that archeologists from all parts of what was once the Roman Empire met in Paris for a conference on mosaic studies called by the *Centre national de la recherche scientifique* and, aware of the lack of co-ordination even within research limited to that epoch, resolved to form an international association for the study of classical mosaics, and to build up a corpus of publications. Similarly, many modern practitioners of mosaic, working away in the isolation of their studios, have never heard of each other, and have never come together to organize associations or exhibitions: those in Ravenna hardly know about developments in London or Los Angeles, and there was an excellent artist living in Rome who had never been to see his colleagues in the famous Vatican workshop across the Tiber. The alchemists who manufacture the coloured *smalti* according to a basic formula which has remained unchanged for more than two thousand years tend to keep their mixtures and methods secret from the prying eyes of those outside their companies. It is for reasons like these that mosaic, for all its great splendour and wide geographic diffusion, is today the least appreciated of the arts.

This in itself is reason enough for trying to take a comprehensive view of the art of mosaic. If the picture cannot be complete or perfect, the conspectus of all periods and all regions may well yield insights not obtainable within a smaller compass. Some unsolved mysteries of ancient finds might come nearer solution if scholars took a closer look at the practical procedures of living mosaicists; and these in turn might benefit from the researches of archaeologists. There is also a gap to be filled in the five-thousand-year history of the art by carrying it right up to the present time: a time which, after the two great phases of mosaic in classical antiquity and in the Christian Middle Ages, sees its third flowering, presenting more varied facets than ever before.

Today this ancient art is in fact one of the most contemporary as well, for, by its very nature, it has close affinities with modern styles, and the present-day world is particularly well equipped both to develop and to apply its potentialities. Mosaic calls for simplification and stylization. It encourages striking effects and a heightening of reality; it inclines towards expressionistic vigour and abstract shapes. It practised *pointillisme* and Op Art thousands of years before Seurat or Vasarely, and it has always embraced the principles of collage, of montage, of the *objet trouvé*. It can find opportunities in contemporary architecture, adding life to plain wall spaces without interfering with the idea of functional building, while, on the other hand, modern technology provides new materials which, though not always improving the art of mosaic, can often make it less expensive and help it to expand. Becoming democratic and secular after fifteen centuries in the almost exclusive service of the Church, it can once again add colour to our daily life, as it did in Roman times.

What is necessary is that mosaic should be appreciated and applied as a medium in its own right, governed by its own laws of style, and the first requirement, if one is to understand the nature of these laws, is to define the nature of mosaic. Unfortunately, the origin of the word is uncertain, and fails to provide a useful clue. Some have tried to link it etymologically with the Arabic *muzáuwaq* ('decorated'); however, mosaic was not invented by the Arabs but was imported by them from Byzantium, along with its usual Arabic name *fusáifisâ'* which is in fact derived from the Greek *psephos* ('small stone' or 'pebble'). It seems much safer to trace mosaic back to the Muses – the word as much as the art it denotes. Safer, but not proved, because the Greek terms *mousaikon*, *mouseion*, etc., do not occur until very late, mainly in Byzantine times, when they had apparently been re-imported from Latin. To confuse things even further, the Romans, in the great period of their mosaics, had no generic term for them, making do with the word *tessera* or *tessella* to denote an individual little mosaic cube, and with composite phrases such as *pavimentum tesseris structum* (a floor constructed from cubes). Pliny the Elder (*Hist. nat.* XXXVI 184–189) uses the Greek word *lithostroton* (literally, 'stone spread') for a type of floor which cannot now be identified with certainty but which, he says, 'began already under Sulla' and 'drove out the *pavimenta*'. It is not until around AD 300, in the biographies by the *Scriptores Historiae Augustae*, that one comes across the phrase '*pictura est de museo*', and a century later St Augustine mentions figures which '*musivo picta sunt*'. In the vernaculars of the Middle Ages, this word recurs in a variety of guises: *mousaique*, *musycke*, *musaico*, *mosaick*, etc.

However, to come to a working definition, a mosaic is a coherent pattern or image in which each component element is built up from small regular or irregular pieces of substances such as stone, glass or ceramic, held in place by plaster, entirely or predominantly covering a plane or curved surface, even a three-dimensional shape, and normally integrated with its architectural context.

The definition has to be somewhat laborious if it is to embrace manifestations such as mosaic relief, mosaic sculpture and mixed techniques which have developed only recently but are perfectly consistent with the nature of mosaic. At the same time it must exclude a number of similar and related techniques which differ essentially from mosaic. One of these is inlay, in which small fragments or larger pieces are cut to shape and fitted together, without leaving any gaps, on a plane surface, usually of wood. Similarly, in classical *opus sectile* pieces of stone or tile are pre-cut in the specific shapes of elements of the design, rather than built up from several anonymous particles as in mosaic proper. The term *opus sectile*, which is used somewhat loosely, covers two types of decoration: on the one hand, geometric patterns assembled from standard units such as bars, diamonds, triangles or hexagons – a technique akin to that developed much later by the Cosmati guild in medieval Rome as a purely ornamental variety of mosaic (*pl. 73*); on the other hand there is a figurative type – not unlike the more recent *pietra dura* or so-called 'Florentine mosaic', a kind of stone inlay in which coherent pictorial elements such as leaves or scrolls are cut out and fitted into the base (*pl. 74*). Similarly, in stained-glass windows a leaf or a helmet consists of a single piece of glass, or of a small number of comparatively large pieces, and it is this fact (rather than its translucency) that distinguishes stained glass from mosaic. Other cousins of mosaic include patterns made of beads, sequins, buttons, bone, nails, seeds, coloured-paper shapes, indeed collages of any kind of material; the feather mosaics worked on cloth which Montezuma, king of the Aztecs, presented to Cortez, the *conquistador*; embroidery, tapestry and patchwork rugs or bedspreads; a flower bed with the blooms laid out in the shape of a coat of arms, or a crowd of people in shirts of different colours forming letters or images. Even the shop-front with coloured tiles in decorative arrangement is a distant relative, though here the large size of the squares excludes one important characteristic of mosaic: the fact that the separate spots of colour, when viewed from a distance, merge on the retina like brush dots in *pointilliste* painting.

This divisionist element is the basis of some of the most admirable achievements of mosaic. This also applies, in a technical sense at least, to soft colour gradations with a modelling effect which bring it close to painting, sometimes making the two barely distinguishable. Mosaic has often been regarded as a more durable form of painting; in fact, many works of Hellenistic and Roman painting are known only from copies in mosaic, and in the eighteenth century most of the paintings in St Peter's were replaced by mosaic reproductions. Domenico Ghirlandaio is said to have dubbed the medium *pittura per l'eternità*: painting for eternity. It is a noble idea, yet a sadly wrong-headed one. For one thing, a mosaic is certainly not as durable as the individual cubes, which so easily become detached. What is worse is that the confusion inherent in Ghirlandaio's phrase has often led to both astounding feats of skill and a disregard for the essential quality of mosaic – that tendency towards stylization which it derives from the coarseness of the particles and the conspicuousness of the interstices between them. This micro-geometric material is used in the most logical and most effective way when shape is sharply juxtaposed with shape and colour with colour, whereas a naturalistic illusion of volume and depth tends to disguise the functional fact that mosaic is a floor or wall decoration rather than a self-contained picture in a frame. As Gino Severini, a painter who understood mosaic, put it in a lecture at Ravenna in 1952: 'No false relief, no false background depth should be shown on walls, and thus no perspective, no volume in *chiaroscuro*; the wall should be decorated, not destroyed; its vertical nature and its plane surface should remain intact.' Of course, an elaborate illusion of depth may well show a more highly skilled technique; and only blinkered theorists will deny that some masterpieces of this kind are expressive and impressive works of art, livelier and richer than some more rudimentary ones which stick strictly to the rule of flatness. The conflict between flatness and depth pervades the history of the medium and has often been a stimulus. It is possible to reconcile the two by breaking down the shapes and colours of the motif in something like the manner of a late Cézanne painting. When a balance is struck between them – that is often a mark of perfection.

Apart from differentiating between mosaic and other similar media, a distinction has to be made between two types of mosaic which almost amount to separate media: floor mosaic (prevalent in classical times) and wall and ceiling mosaic (prevalent in the Middle Ages). Practical purposes determine their respective aesthetic rules and techniques – a difference rather like that between those other two sisters, the theatre and the cinema. A floor has to be firm and smooth, both in material and in fitting; and, since it is normally viewed from eye-level, there is scope for a display of intricate detail. A wall or ceiling mosaic, on the other hand, not being exposed to walking feet, can be made of less robust stuff and does not have to present a smooth surface, so that pieces can be set at differing angles, or even on different planes; moreover, since it is almost invariably seen from some distance, fine detail would be lost, and bold stylization will have the greater effect.

In either case, a mosaic, laboriously assembled from thousands of tiny fragments, is an expensive type of decoration. It needs a patron rich enough to have his building embellished in this costly way, so that the client is bound to have greater influence on its choice of subject, as well as its style, than he does in most other arts. Royalty and the Church, endeavouring to obtain from this majestic medium the greatest splendour for their authority, have sustained its greatest splendour. This is why mosaic usually represents the dominant aspects of the political, intellectual, social and economic conditions of an epoch. In subject matter as well as in style, it prefers consolidation and consummation to experiment and exploration. Being so cumbersome technically, it is slow to change and tends to limp behind the stylistic evolution going on in other arts. In its striving for perfection it has little time to be progressive.

The artist has to be familiar with a complex technique if he is to make full use of its manifold potentialities; a good design on paper does not guarantee a good mosaic. As a result of the blurring of the line between mosaic and painting, painters have all too frequently been thought automatically competent to design mosaics. But a painter does not normally sense in his pencil or brush the formal properties peculiar to those little coloured cubes; and, even when a mosaicist has done his best to translate the painter's cartoon into his own medium, the result is not necessarily an ideal mosaic. Close collaboration of the designing painter with the practical mosaicist can be a good substitute – but still no more than a substitute – for the ideal which should once again become the rule: the identity of the artist with the artisan.

What is equally important is close collaboration between the mosaic artist and the architect. The mosaicist should not see his work as an independent microcosm but should bear its architectural role in mind. The architect should include any mosaic decoration and its function when he is drawing up his plans, rather than add it as an afterthought when dreary patches seem to cry out for something to give them life. The mosaic's colour and lines may crucially modify the lines and the spatial effect of a building. The decoration may work against the architecture, as happens only too often, but it can also help to emphasize the shape of the building and of its parts, to define and divide an undefined and undivided surface, to underline the character of the building, achieving an effect not obtainable by architecture alone but only by a *Gesamtkunstwerk* in which architecture and mosaic are harmoniously integrated.

I PIAZZA ARMERINA, Sicily. *c.* AD 300. Dimensions of detail about 2 x 2.50 m.
The bison from the 70 m.-long Great Hunt mosaic in this late Roman villa – possibly a country residence of Emperor Maximianus Herculius – displays a colourful vitality which suggests the influence of the mosaic style of the Roman province of Africa.

II PIAZZA ARMERINA, Sicily. Fourth century AD. Roughly life-size.
Roman girl athletes wearing briefs (*subligaria*) and bikini tops in the 'Sala delle dieci ragazze'. The floor of this room originally had a geometric pattern, but this was covered a few decades later with a pictorial pavement arranged in two rows, or 'registers', and representing ten young women engaged in various sports.

I

II

1 Ur, Iraq. The so-called 'Mosaic Standard of Ur' (detail). *c.* 2500 BC. British Museum, London.
Sumerian object of unknown purpose. Figures in cut and incised shell, surrounded by mosaic of lapis lazuli, limestone and shell, mounted on a high-gabled wooden box measuring 22 x 47 cm. The illustration shows part of the panel depicting war.

2 El-'ubaid, Iraq. Sumerian column (restored). *c.* 2600 BC. British Museum, London.
Originally a palm log covered with black, white and red mosaic in limestone and mother-of-pearl.

3 Uruk (modern Warka), Iraq. Sumerian façade. *c.* 3000 BC. Staatliche Museen, East Berlin.
Half-columns with various three-tone patterns formed by clay pegs set in mud. In this earliest instance of a mosaic technique, mosaic is already used as an integral part of architecture, decorating as well as strengthening it.

4 Olynthos, Chalcidice peninsula: House of Good Fortune. Bellerophon, mounted on Pegasus, fighting the Chimera. *c.* 415 BC. Diameter of pavement, about 300 cm.; of central panel, 130 cm.
Dark and light-coloured pebbles set in pale brown mortar.

5 Pella, Macedonia. Deer hunt. *c.* 320 BC. Pictorial panel 310 x 310 cm., surrounded by two borders.
Pebble mosaic with the artist's signature: Gnosis. Excavated 1961.

6 Delos: House of the Masks. Mythological figure (possibly Dionysos) in female attire riding a panther. Probably from the first half of the second century BC. Marble, onyx, agate and smalti. Pictorial panel (*emblema*) about 100 x 100 cm.
Rich colours set against black background.

7 Tivoli: Hadrian's Villa. Drinking pigeons. Probably AD 117/138 or else late Republic (first century BC). 85 x 98 cm. (including border). Museo Capitolino, Rome.
Regarded as a version of the pigeons mosaic by Sosos of Pergamon (second century BC) which served as a model for many similar designs in Christian times (cf. *pl. 43*). The wide margin in dating is indicative of the fact that Greek models continued to be copied over a long period. Small, closely-fitting tesserae, highly polished surface.

8 Rome. Detail of the so-called ἀσάρωτος οἶκος ('unswept floor' after a meal) from the Aventine. Second century AD. Dimensions of detail about 30 x 40 cm. Vatican Museum, Rome (formerly in the Lateran Museum).
A copy or imitation of a famous work by Sosos of Pergamon (second century BC).

9 Pergamon. Signature of the artist Hephaistion on a simulated scrap of papyrus, detail of a pavement in the palace of King Eumenes. First half of the second century BC. Dimensions of detail about 15 x 20 cm. Staatliche Museen, East Berlin.
This pavement, possibly the earliest instance of the use of smalti (in combination with natural stone), is of very high quality; but the artist's personal joke is symptomatic of the development towards illusionism.

10 Pompeii or Herculaneum. The Three Graces. Before AD 79. About 100 x 75 cm. Museo Archeologico Nazionale, Naples.
Not polished, and thus probably a mural. Surviving parts of background dark blue. The lines of tesserae are used to delineate muscles more clearly than in the corresponding painting (*pl. 11*).

11 Pompeii. The Three Graces. Before AD 79. About 75 x 60 cm. Museo Archeologico Nazionale, Naples.
One of the four surviving Pompeian fresco paintings of this subject. Light and shade are used to model curves more clearly than in the corresponding mosaic (*pl. 10*).

12 Pompeii. Female portrait (so-called 'Sappho'). Perhaps late Hellenistic (*c.* first century BC). About 40 x 30 cm. Museo Archeologico Nazionale, Naples.

13 Fayyûm, Egypt. Hellenistic mummy portait, painted on wood. About 60 x 30 cm. Louvre, Paris.

14–15 Cologne. Dionysos mosaic on the floor of a banqueting-hall. Probably *c.* AD 220. Marble, limestone, slate, *terra sigillata* (red), glass (blue and green). 10.57 x 7 m.
A system of squares, some of which are superimposed upon others to form eight-pointed stars, encloses thirty-one pictorial panels which resemble Greek *emblemata* (though probably not sharing their technique of separate execution). Panels near edges depict birds, oysters and fruit; those in the centre, scenes from the

Dionysos myth, among them *pl. 14*, Pan with goat; *pl. 15*, young Silenus with syrinx (shepherd's pipe). White backgrounds in fan arrangement of tesserae (instead of *opus tessellatum*). Discovered 1941 during excavations for an air-raid shelter on the south side of Cologne Cathedral.

16 NENNIG, Saarland. Gladiators and umpire. Third century AD. One of the largest of the nine (or seven surviving) pictorial panels of a pavement measuring 10.3 x 15.65 m.

17 POMPEII: the so-called 'Villa of Cicero'. Itinerant musicians on a stage. *c.* 100 BC. 43 x 41 cm. Museo Archeologico Nazionale, Naples.

One of two *emblemata* bearing the signature of Dioscurides of Samos. Probably based on a painting of the third century BC. One of the best and most celebrated works of classical mosaic which follows a painterly style while adapting it sensitively to the technique of mosaic.

18 BOSCÉAZ, near Orbe, Switzerland. Fragmentary pavement representing weekly deities. First quarter of third century AD. 460 x 425 cm.

Cosmological and mythological motifs, probably based on a design for a painted stucco ceiling.

19–21 POMPEII. House of the Faun. Alexander mosaic. End of the second century BC. 342 x 592 cm. (including borders). Museo Archeologico Nazionale, Naples. This most famous of all classical mosaics shows Alexander (left) and Darius (right) at the moment when the Persian king's battle-chariot is turning in flight. A number of inconsistencies, which are noticed on closer inspection of the dramatic composition, have been used to support the hypothesis that the 'indirect' system of setting was known in classical times (see p. 46). Natural stone and some smalti; four principal colours: white, black, red, yellow.

22 OSTIA: Mithraeum of the Imperial Palace. Silvanus. Third century AD. Height of mosaic niche 157 cm. Vatican Museum, Rome (formerly in the Lateran Museum).

The blue and white nimbus is reminiscent of the Good Shepherd. Background dark blue and green. (The inscriptions commemorate restoration work carried out under Pope Pius IX.)

23 POMPEII: House of the Large Fountain. Nymphaeum (mosaic fountain). Before AD 79. About 350 x 200 cm. Mainly glass tesserae (in nine colours, not polished) decorated with rows of shells.

24 ROME. Coloured head of Medusa in round medallion diameter 46 cm.), surrounded by black-and-white geometric ornament reminiscent of modern Op Art. Second century AD. Museo Nazionale Romano (delle Terme), Rome.

25 POMPEII. *Cave canem.* (Beware of the dog.) Before AD 79. 63 x 61 cm. Museo Archeologico Nazionale, Naples.

Black on a white ground, with only the tongue and collar in red. The sequence of operations is particularly evident in this work: 1. black figure, 2. white tesserae along outlines of figure, 3. background area in straight rows (*opus tessellatum*). (There is a similar dog mosaic at the entrance to the House of the Tragic Poet in Pompeii.)

26 ROME. Skeletal figure with the Greek motto 'Know Thyself'. Late first or early second century AD. 186 x 171 cm. Museo Nazionale Romano (delle Terme), Rome.

Black and white only.

27 OSTIA: Fire Brigade Barracks. Bull sacrifice. Late second or early third century AD. Width of detail about 350 cm.

Excellent example of the Roman black-and-white style, of which Ostia contains a particularly rich collection. An impression of modelling is achieved by the graphic means of white lines within the black figures.

28 CARTHAGE, Tunisia. Coronation of Aphrodite. Fourth century AD. 150 x 240 cm. Musée National du Bardo, Tunis.

29 DOUGGA, Tunisia: House of Ulysses and Dionysos. Ulysses and the Sirens. Third century AD. About 300 x 200 cm. Musée National du Bardo, Tunis.

Typical of the Roman-African style of mosaic: lively, anecdotal, colourful, related to the aesthetic traditions of the ancient Orient (wavy line symbolizing water).

30 ANTIOCH: House of the Buffet Supper. Centauromachy (detail of frieze). AD 193/235.

Grey-yellow on red ground with black shades. Soft impressionistic style of superb quality.

31 ANTIOCH: House of the Evil Eye. The 'lucky hunchback'. Inscription: 'You too.' Before AD 115.

The name given to the house by archaeologists is derived from a mosaic showing a magic eye. The sticks held by the hunchback are interpreted by Doro Levi as talismans.

32 ANTIOCH: House of the Evil Eye. The infant Hercules strangling serpents. Before AD 115.

One of the numerous classical representations of this mythological subject.

33 ISTANBUL: Great Palace of the Byzantine Emperors. Male head among acanthus scrolls in the border of the pavement in the north eastern palace. Date uncertain, probably early sixth century.

Marble and other types of rock in many colours on a white background. Last splendour of classical mosaic. (For other scrolls cf. *pls 39–41*.)

1

2

3

4

5

6

7

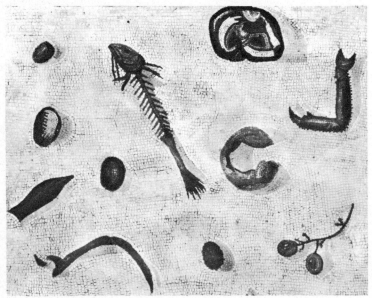

8

9

10

11

13

12

14

15

16

17

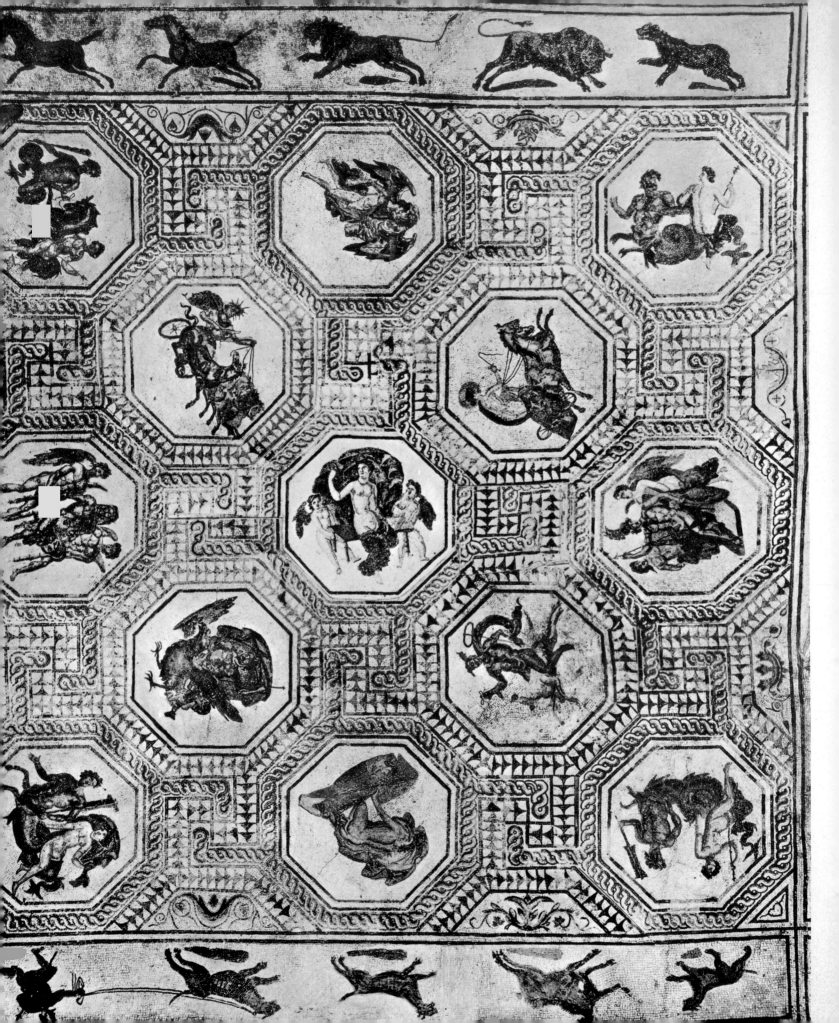

19

20

21

22

23

24

25

26

27

28

29

30

31   32

33

First Phase: Classical Pavements

The birth of mosaic art can be seen when children press pebbles and shells into the sandy beach and discover that the various hues can be laid out to form patterns or pictures. This happens so naturally that it may be regarded as one of the basic inventions, as old as that of cooking. Very early man may have used this simple method to make a firm floor in his cave or hut and, in doing so, may even have pierced the grey dawn of civilization with a first bright flicker of art. When one thinks of existing cave paintings, prehistoric mosaics seem quite conceivable – but, of course, they would have been washed away the waters of thousands of years.

This may be why the very oldest mosaics that have survived are not in fact pavements but wall decorations – an invention not quite so obvious, and therefore presumably representing a more advanced stage of development. In fact, the material used in them is not a natural one, like stone, but a manufactured product: baked clay. An early Sumerian frontage, more than eighty feet long and dating from the end of the fourth millennium BC, which has been unearthed in the Eanna sanctuary at Uruk (modern Warka) is completely studded with conical clay pegs between one and a half and six inches long, their points embedded in the mud wall, reinforcing and decorating it at the same time (*pl. 3*). The visible ends are often coloured in black, red or white tones, and some have white rims standing out around a circular depression which is darkened by shadow. The wall consists of a series of shallow half-columns, each with its own geometric motif: zigzag bands, triangles, lozenges. The resemblance to plaiting or weaving patterns has led to the hypothesis that they were intended to be more durable versions of wall hangings. There are analogous theories which link the checkerboard pattern of early pebble mosaics with even earlier two-tone brick floors; or certain designs on subsequent mosaic pavements with rug designs; or the rosette ornaments of later periods with designs common in embroidery or inlay. However this may be, the inspiration may well have been mutual. The derivation of certain ornamental motifs is hardly sufficient evidence for the origin of the technique of mosaic.

These long cones of clay, and later of stone, which were driven into Mesopotamian mud walls are different technically from flat tablets, or *tesserae*, those basic units of mosaic as we now know it. But clay cones firmly driven into the plaster,

33

rather than just adhering to its surface, would seem to be a less obvious method, and may perhaps be supposed to have been an improvement on earlier little tablets of stone or bone, with the added advantage that they were easier to prepare in large quantities.

The earliest known examples of tesserae date from the early dynastic period III in nearby Ur (*c.* 2600 BC). Drinking vessels, wands and other small objects from the Sumerian 'Royal Cemetery' there bear ornamental bands of square or triangular fragments of shell, bone, lapis lazuli and red limestone or paste, arranged in alternating colours. Another find of similar date is the box-like, gabled object which Sir Leonard Woolley named the 'Standard of Ur', although its purpose remains obscure (*pl. 1*). The incrustations on its four sides have geometric borders, again assembled from triangular tesserae of blue lapis lazuli, white shell and red limestone. Lapis lazuli mosaic, a patchwork of random fragments this time, also fills in the background of the pictorial scenes. The white shell silhouettes of men and animals, however, are cut as figures complete in themselves, rather than pieced together from fragments. The artists, it seems, still lacked the confidence to tackle the intricacies of figurative mosaic. How close they were to this next step can be seen in several somewhat larger friezes from the temple of El 'Ubaid near Ur with similar silhouette figures, some of which are composed of a number of pieces of white limestone or shell; but each piece is shaped separately to represent a complete unit, such as the head, torso or legs. In the same place and around the same time, 2600 BC, tablet mosaic made its first appearance in an architectural context. Palm-log columns were covered with thin tesserae, some square, some wedge-shaped, made of black bituminous limestone, white mother-of-pearl and pink limestone in a three-colour scheme typical of early Sumerian art (*pl. 2*). The tesserae were fastened by copper wire to a base of bitumen, some of which oozed up through the joints, emphasizing the separating character of these interstices – an essential feature of mosaic art. These finds, assembled in a small room of the British Museum, must silence any doubt or argument about the fact that the history of mosaic does indeed stretch back five thousand years.

Not that it developed in an unbroken line. The clear-cut tesserae of the Sumerians fell into oblivion, and eventually gross pebbles took their place. It was not until two thousand years later that Greeks returned to the idea of cutting mosaic stones in well-defined shapes and sizes. Even then, and throughout antiquity, mosaic facing on columns, or indeed on any other vertical surface, was very rare until, in the early Christian era, mosaic ascended again from floor to walls.

Pharaonic Egypt did not produce anything which can properly be classed as mosaic. Some of the walls in the tomb of King Zoser at Saqqâra (*c.* 2750 BC) are covered in fairly large and slightly curved greenish tiles imitating the weave of rush matting, and comparable techniques occur in buildings of later centuries; but this is not mosaic. Curiously, Egyptian 'faïence' is not fired clay, as the term normally suggests today, but sand heated with natron, and thus not very different from the *smalti* which, thousands of years later, were to become the most glorious of all mosaic materials. However, the Egyptians never broke this 'faïence' up into fragments to be arranged in polychrome combinations. They did use it for exquisite inlay work, and one such, a fourth-century-BC sarcophagus lid in the Turin museum, has in fact been quoted as a work of mosaic; but while, for example, a bird is indeed composed of pieces of different colours, each individual feather is treated as an autonomous unit, rather than assembled from fragments as it would be in true mosaic.

Meanwhile, mosaic pavements slowly evolved in western Asia. A crude type of pavement of natural pebbles, not yet arranged in patterns, had been known as early as the third millennium BC at Mari on the middle Euphrates, and later at Carchemish as well. Not far away, in the late Assyrian royal palaces of Til-Barsib and Arslan-Tash, dating from the ninth and eighth centuries BC, there are pavements made of alternating black and white pebbles forming concentric circles surrounded by squares. They can be called mosaics, although they are hardly more than cobblestones in a decorative layout. A three-colour design in pebbles – white, blue and dark red – occurs in the eighth and seventh centuries BC at Gordion. As the Phrygian city was destroyed and reconstructed soon afterwards, the Greeks cannot have seen this pavement when they arrived with Alexander, but by that time their countrymen had long been familiar with mosaic in the Aegean world. There is nothing to prove that they had been influenced by Asia, though, equally, nothing to prove that they had not.

In Crete, crude pebble floors without a pattern had been known in neolithic times and, later, in the Minoan period. Some small triangles made of various metals and semi-precious stones, which Sir Arthur Evans found in a stone box at Knossos, have been tentatively interpreted as material for delicate mosaic work, a suggestion which, in the absence of any completed mosaics in Crete, must seem unlikely.

Greek Pebble Mosaics

In early Greece, too, floors had been made of pebbles, ground smooth by the waters of rivers or seas, and embedded in mortar. The earliest evidence of a design occurs in the scant remains of a floor in the sixth-century-BC temple of Athena Pronaia at Delphi. It was in the same epoch, when Greek genius was establishing the classic forms of architecture and sculpture, that it used these humble pebbles to evolve mosaic as a fine art. In that sense Pliny, though unaware of Middle Eastern archaeology, was right in saying that, 'Paved floors (*pavimenta*) skilfully executed in the way of a painting originated with the Greeks.'

In the earliest phase, designs consisted of geometric and floral ornaments, usually black and white, but sometimes including coloured pebbles. Late in the fifth century BC the first figure scenes appeared, mostly of animals fighting. Sites include Athens, Corinth and Motya, a Phoenician settlement in western Sicily where oriental figures coexist rather strangely with Greek ornamental borders. Particularly numerous and particularly fine are the excellently preserved pebble mosaics at Olynthos in the Chalcidice peninsula. Moreover, the city's destruction by Philip of Macedonia in 348 BC provides a *terminus ante quem* to act as a sheet anchor for dating, a task which is often riddled with uncertainties when there are only technical and stylistic clues to go on. David M. Robinson, the excavator, has dated some of the Olynthos pavements as early as 420/410. Among them is the best-known of all, the earliest known complete representation of a mythological scene: Bellerophon on his winged charger, hunting down the Chimera (*pl. 4*).

There is no reason to think that the mosaics found at Olynthos were the first of their kind. The fact that they adorned private houses implies that the art may well have already gone through an earlier phase in the exclusivity of temples and palaces, and a style as sophisticated as this is unlikely to have sprung fully-armed from the head of Zeus. They are exquisite. These gross pebbles in their limited range of hues, strikingly separated by spaces of brown mortar, have engendered a stylization typical of mosaic, and not often achieved again with such simple power and clarity, even with the improved skills of later ages. The figures, in white or buff, are silhouetted against a background of darker pebbles: black, dark blue, green, mauve, or, occasionally, dark red or pink. Apparently the mosaicist laid the outlines first, and then proceeded to fill the space between with white stones in random order, except for details such as the lines of drapery which are indicated by darker pieces. It is a two-dimensional, graphic style that draws its strength from tonal contrast and seems to have been inspired by Greek vase painting. In the ornamental borders which surround or divide the floors, the principal motifs of classical pavements are already present: meanders and wave-crest bands, palmettes and diamonds, vine and laurel leaves. Olynthos is a preview and prospectus of the grammar of Greek art.

Pella, fairly close in both space and time, represents the next step: a movement towards brighter colours and a growing interest in plasticity (*pl. 5*). The excavations begun in 1957 in the royal capital of Macedonia that was Alexander's birthplace presently yielded a number of mosaics, again in private dwellings, which lend colour to the legend of Zeuxis, the Athenian painter working at the court of Pella towards the end of the fifth century BC: he is reputed to have been the first to use light and shade to achieve a three-dimensional effect, and is said to have turned out pictures so realistic that birds swooped down to peck greedily at his painted grapes. Of course, pictures made of pebbles can hardly be sufficiently illusionistic to perform that trick. But there is the intriguing hypothesis that a mosaic showing Dionysos on a panther's back might be based on a lost painting by the famous artist. In fact the Pella mosaics are clearly concerned with modelling, which is done either by very skilfully indicating muscles in thin lines of darker stones (though not black ones, as at Olynthos), or by areas of shadow

III BACCANO: Villa of Septimius Severus. Charioteers of the four circus 'factions'. *c.* AD 200. Each panel 50 x 50 cm. Museo Nazionale Romano (delle Terme), Rome.
The subject exemplifies the lively catholicity of Roman mosaic art. The figures, composed in *opus vermiculatum*, were clearly set first, and the background, in regular rows of *opus tessellatum*, was filled in later. The illusionistic treatment includes the use of shadows.

IV ROME: S. Costanza. *c.* AD 350.
This first major vault mosaic marks the end of the classical era. Exclusively classical and pagan motifs – from the vintage and the cult of Dionysos – are used in this early Christian mausoleum. The barrel vaulting of the 12 ft-wide circular arcade opens at the entrance with geometric ornaments in the manner of Roman pavements, and gains more and more life and movement as one section succeeds the next, reaching sumptuous brilliance at the back of the rotunda. The background is composed of white marble tesserae and the figures are of smalti, including gold smalti.

IV

creating the illusion of volume, just as Zeuxis is said to have done. However this may be, these floors were not laid until around 300 BC, long after his lifetime, and indeed after the death of Alexander who, in a mosaic from the room adjoining the Dionysos scene, is pictured as a young hero tackling a lion. Another hunting subject, of slightly later date to judge by its style, bears the inscription: 'Γνωσις εποησεν'. This Gnosis was presumably the artist who physically produced the mosaic rather than its designer. The designer and the practical mosaicist cannot have been identical, for the two hunting scenes are so similar, in composition as well as in the postures of the figures, that either the second must be derived from the first or, more likely, both are based on a common source (presumably a painting, because painterly handling is even more noticeably imitated in the second of the two). If this deduction is correct, this is an early instance of the practice, so frequent in mosaics, of lifting a motif from painting.

This is also consistent with the move towards more varied colours, which pebbles would hardly seem to encourage. Even the background is not black, but is composed of a *mélange* of blue, green and grey pebbles which combine with the grey mortar to produce an overall pastel tone. The figures still stand out as white silhouettes, but no longer in strict profile. An unusual feature at Pella is the fact that outlines and some details are often sharply delineated by the insertion of strips of lead. They may originally have been used as working aids, for occasionally, as in Pergamon, grooves have been discovered in the mortar bed which were evidently left behind by such strips; and at Delos a template for shaping a common ornamental motif has actually survived. At Pella, however, these metal lines are given an artistic function in the composition – a device of which there are similar, though rare, examples in subsequent periods up to the present day. Another novel feature found at Pella (and a surprising one in these mosaics, which are basically conceived like two-tone pictures) is the practice of picking out details, such as hair, in red, yellow or other brightly-coloured pebbles, creating an effect not unlike that of hand-coloured photographs. It is a mixed style, inventive if not entirely consistent – a new approach not often paralleled in later ages. Throughout the subsequent twenty-two centuries and their stylistic sea changes, mosaic has been governed by a fixed technical formula that had been established in Greece. It may be no accident that these new departures were attempted in Macedonia, a borderland of Hellenic civilization, just as in our own day it is more often outside the traditional homeground of mosaic that unorthodox experiments are undertaken.

The Birth of the Tessera

The mosaics at Pella, made up of pebbles half an inch or less in diameter, were much more elaborate than the earlier ones at Olynthos, where nearly fist-sized stones were used. At roughly the same period mosaic took a further step towards that technique which was to become its classic one. In the vestibule of the temple of Zeus at Olympia, the floors of which are datable to around 325 BC, pebbles are no longer used exclusively in their water-worn natural state: some have been roughly cut or chipped into smaller pieces for greater precision in rendering details like the eyes of a Triton. This method soon became more widespread;

if the craftsman was going to go to the trouble of giving his raw material a preliminary treatment, it was much more convenient to choose larger and more varied stones with a surface that would not cause the hammer or chisel to slip, as happened with round pebbles, and to prepare beforehand a fairly large supply of fragments of standard dimensions and with a level face. Floors assembled from such stone fragments were not as rough as pebble floors (which nevertheless, being cheap, coexisted with them for a long time). They were flat and even, and could be ground and waxed to reveal the colours of the stones in all their brilliance. Mosaic was no longer restricted to the limited palette that pebbles had to offer, but was able to choose from the colours of all types of rock, marble and semi-precious stones. The tessera, invented and used by the Sumerians once before, had been born again among the Greeks.

The earliest mosaic decoration mentioned in classical literature graced a state ship which Hieron II of Syracuse (275–215 BC) had built, under the supervision of Archimedes, as a gift for Ptolemy III (246–221 BC) – just as some ocean liners and luxury yachts in the twentieth century have been adorned with mosaic. According to Athenaeus, who lived in Rome around AD 200 but quotes an earlier author named Moschion, the ship's cabin 'had a floor composed of little tablets of every kind of stone, on which the whole story of the Iliad was wondrously set out'. This clearly refers to polychrome tessera mosaics, and the admiring language suggests that the technique was still novel at the time. It may even be that this new method was perfected in Sicily, for in the centre of the island, at Morgantina (modern Serra Orlando), there is a house dating from the decade 260/250 BC which shows a transitional phase: no longer pebbles, but roughly-hewn polychrome stones, together with some red terracotta fragments. They are irregular both in size and shape, but for some details, such as the eyes, they are cut specifically to shape, and the surface of the mosaic is polished.

In the magnificent mosaics on the island of Delos – of uncertain date but probably from the first half of the second century BC – the transition to carefully cut polychrome stone cubes is complete, and so is the emergence of the Hellenistic style. In many cases the backgrounds are still black, although Delos also has some white backgrounds, anticipating the preference of the Roman Imperial era. But the mysterious figure in female attire riding a panther (pl. 6) glows richly in twenty colours or more, and is positively baroque in posture, costume and modelling. An oriental influence may have been at work; in fact, there are some Delos mosaics which bear the signature of an artist from Syria, one Asklepiades of Arados. But there is an important secret behind the gorgeous display of colour: the fact that, together with various kinds of marble and semi-precious stones such as onyx and agate, *smalti* have been used.

Smalti – the bits of coloured glass produced by fusing sand and mineral oxides (pp. 142–4) – were eventually to become, on the walls of churches in Rome and Ravenna, the mosaic material *par excellence*. Their range of colours is unlimited. Throughout the Greek and Roman epoch, however, smalti in rich reds and greens or other colours were only used to fill gaps in the spectrum of colours provided by natural stones. For the time being, stone retained its dominance, being the more hard-wearing material and so more suitable for pavements, which make up virtually all of the immense wealth of mosaics left by the classical world.

At the time of the Delos pavements, or possibly a little later, smalti also appear on Asian soil, in the admirable, though fragmentary, mosaics of the second-century royal citadel of Pergamon. The artists of Pergamon seem to have been the first to superimpose one colour on another to create an intermediate shade: a particularly bright red was obtained by applying a translucent coat of red plaster to white tesserae – a similar procedure was later to become a standard practice in the manufacture of gold smalti (p. 144). Even more important for stylistic development was the minute size of the tesserae, some of which were as small as pin-heads. The use of particles so tiny permitted designs so detailed and delicate that mosaic was now able to conceal the fact that it was an assemblage of separate pieces – to make believe that it was not mosaic at all – and it began to revel in this rather perverse perfectionism. A Pergamon artist, Hephaistion, contrived to sign his name, in hard stone, on what looks like a casual scrap of papyrus, stuck down with blobs of red wax and dog-eared at one corner (*pl. 9*). This amusing little *trompe l'œil* is truly a business-card advertising a master illusionist's skill; but it is a skill that denies the essential nature of the medium. On the very threshold of its artistic advance the newly-won technical perfection of mosaic is pointing the way to its artistic decline. This is the paradox of the greatness and tragedy of mosaic art.

This city was also the home of the artist whom Pliny knew as the most famous among mosaicists, Sosos of Pergamon. Two of his compositions, mentioned by Pliny, have survived in Italy in several copies or adaptations. One of them is another piece of illusionism: the so called ἀσάρωτος οἶκος (*pl. 8*), an 'unswept floor' apparently littered with fish bones, nutshells, fruit stalks and other remains of a feast that seem to lie and cast their shadows upon a surface of which they are in fact part. The other Sosos motif, hardly less naturalistic, is the picture of drinking pigeons, perched on the rim of a bowl (*pl. 7*) – an image later absorbed and spiritualized in the iconography of Christian mosaic.

The photographic, indeed almost stereographic, illusionism of the Pergamon artists and all those who followed in their footsteps is achieved by making very small tesserae, in carefully graded shades of each colour, perform gradual transitions of tone, gently modelling the object with its highlights and shadows. The technical affinity with painting is obvious. The stylistic affinity can be appreciated by comparing, for example, the Roman female portrait in mosaic at Naples with a painted mummy portrait from Hellenistic Egypt (*pls 12–13*). Many mosaics of classical times are, in fact, copies after Greek and Roman paintings. This is made strikingly clear by a look at popular subjects such as the Three Graces (*pls 10–11*) which, apart from frequent treatment in sculpture, are extant both as paintings (in four versions from Pompeii alone) and as mosaics (from Herculaneum as well as from Barcino in Spain). Many other paintings would have been lost for ever and there would be many more blank pages in the history of Greek and Roman painting but for this method of 'painting for eternity'.

The handmaiden's service that the art of mosaic thus rendered to the art of painting was no doubt a virtue. Nor need one doubt that mosaic, by following models conceived in terms of liquid paint rather than of stones, found its way to some superb achievements – of art as well as of craftsmanship. Nevertheless it was the wrong road, because it frequently led mosaic away from the line of development marked out for it by the angular nature of its own peculiar material. The right road, as well as the difference between the two arts, can be clearly seen by comparing Pompeian painting, which is more involved with the articulation of space and soft painterly detail, with Pompeian mosaics, which, even when adapted from painted originals, are adapted in terms of mosaic and speak in the starker idiom of their medium.

This is true of the Three Graces mosaic, although the work is not particularly delicate and, incidentally, seems to be an early wall mosaic, for the surface is not ground smooth as it is in all contemporary pavements. There is little variation in the tan flesh-tints; the curves of the three bodies are rather suggested by the *andamento* (deliberate 'coursing' of the tesserae and the joints between them), which emphasizes the length of the legs and the roundness of the knee-caps. Draperies, too, can be shaped and enlivened by this subtle stylistic device, as can be seen in the exquisite little comedy scene of itinerant musicians (*pl. 17*). This is apparently based on a third-century-BC painting, although the mosaic from Pompeii was probably not produced until about 100 BC, and is one of two signed with the name Dioscurides of Samos – who was presumably the mosaicist rather than the original painter, but must be ranked as a major artist on any terms. Another device he uses is that of rendering colour not by following the assorted shades of the actual colours present but by expressionistic means: in the robes, the highlighted parts in brilliant yellow and white are boldly contrasted with the blue and black of the shadowed portions – rather like the *cangiantismo* in mannerist painting of the cinquecento. Dioscurides thinks so completely in terms of colour that there is hardly a trace of linear design. Yet, however plastic the effect of the figures, the composition of the mosaic (and perhaps of its painted original as well) is not very successful in handling depth and placing the figures in space. The two-dimensional art of antiquity cared little for this problem; it usually let figures float in an anonymous void, or perch on a narrow line or strip of land or water. This may be regarded as a shortcoming; but for tessellated floors it is an advantage – their purpose, after all, is to decorate a level surface, not to obscure the pavement's functional role by creating the illusion of depressions and yawning abysses. In fact, Dioscurides has found an elegant compromise: his scene is set on a stage, the rectangular back wall of which acts as a frame for the picture. The same rectangular shape is echoed in the horizontal rows of tesserae filling the pale background, set in plain *opus tessellatum* (see p. 147) which, being neutral, helps to heighten the lively realism and the gentle caricature of this little masterpiece.

The same period, the late second century BC, also produced the most celebrated ancient mosaic – indeed the most famous ancient painting as well – which is one of the most powerful battle scenes in the history of art. This is the Alexander mosaic which was discovered in the House of the Faun at Pompeii on 24 October 1831 (*pls 19–21*). Goethe, seeing a sketch of it a few days before he died, wrote in prophetic rapture: 'Our own and future ages will not be able to do justice to this marvel of art and, after consideration and examination, we shall be obliged to return again and again to pure and simple admiration.' Admiration for the whirling yet well-balanced composition showing Alexander and Darius in dramatic confrontation; for an economy which uses a mere handful of warriors to suggest enormous armies, and a leafless tree to evoke the bleakness of the battlefield; for the intricacy and accuracy in depicting so many individual fates that reach their culmination at the moment of the clash between the two great powers; and for the elaborate rendering of military equipment and human expression. All this is achieved with various shades of only four principal colours, white and black, red and yellow; there are no blues and greens except in the borders. This seems to make the Alexander mosaic an example of Greek four-colour painting – that technique about which there is so little information.

It may be taken for granted that the scene is derived from a painting, but the identity of the painter has given rise to some speculation, and there are various candidates apart from Philoxenos of Eretria who, according to Pliny (*Hist. nat.* XXXV 110), painted 'Alexander's fight with Darius' for King Kassander of Macedonia (317–297 BC). The painting may have found its way to Rome, perhaps when L. Aemilius Paullus defeated the Macedonians in 168 BC, so that the mosaicists may have been able to work from the original itself rather than from an intermediate copy. But no matter how, when, where or by whom the mosaic was produced, it is clearly Greek art.

Greek artists kept their leading position in both the design and the practice of mosaic throughout the classical world, just as they were to do during the Middle Ages when they carried their skill from Byzantium to Damascus and Palermo, to Córdoba and Kiev. This explains why the focus has imperceptibly shifted from Greece across to Italy. Along with their canon of ornaments and iconography, the Greeks had, even in the early pebble pavements of Olynthos and Pella, been evolving the principles of pavement layout which were to affect the technical procedure of classical mosaic.

Technical Development

The humblest mosaic-type floor decoration, *opus signinum* (named after Signia, a town in Latium), is a levelled surface made up from odd fragments of stone or pottery of different colours, set at random in lime mortar rather like raisins in a cake. It is found, for example, on foot-paths along the streets of Pompeii and in the service rooms of houses – occasionally embellished by simple rows of black stones. It is nothing more than the familiar 'terrazzo' still commonly used today in kitchens and corridors – a craft rather than an art. Nor is there much difference between a humdrum tiled floor and a mosaic with a simple 'all-over' pattern endlessly repeated from wall to wall, like a fitted carpet bought by the square yard. Patterns of this type, too, were developed by the Greeks. But they found greater scope and satisfaction for their sense of form in floor layouts tailored specifically to the shape of the room and articulated in a concentric system. The focal point would be a central medallion, usually depicting a figure or a scene, and surrounded by several bands of abstract or floral ornament; if the floor was a large one, other pictorial motifs and medallions would be grouped between them in a systematic and thematically harmonious arrangement (*pl. 18*). The respective importance of the principal and the subordinate elements in the design was reflected in working procedures.

Laying the background and borders was routine work, sometimes done with the aid of templates and normally involving relatively coarse tesserae (about half an inch square). In the classic technique of *opus tessellatum* these were set in straight lines (as in the background of *pl. 17*), or else in curved lines where these were required by the motif or where it was a matter of filling the awkward corner between an irregularly-shaped figure and the regular background rows. Pictorial portions came to be set in a much more intricate and flexible manner known as *opus vermiculatum* ('worm-shaped work') in which quite small tesserae occasionally only one square millimetre in size and not necessarily square in shape, were set not according to any mechanical system but in an arrangement dictated by the shapes of the figures. The very name for a medallion of this kind, *emblema* (i.e. 'insert'), suggests that this highly delicate work was, as a rule, carried out separately by specialists in the studio and not on the site like the rest of the work. Some of these inserts have been found still mounted on a shallow tray of terracotta or stone embedded in the middle of the pavement. Occasionally these trays have raised edges, flush with the level of the tessellated floor, as in the Dioscurides panel (*pl. 17* and *fig. 14* on p. 141). This leaves no doubt that the *emblema* was portable. In most cases, however, there is no such tray, even if the work has clearly been done separately.

This has given rise to the hypothesis that ancient mosaicists must have already practised the so-called 'indirect', or 'reverse', system of application which is very popular today (p. 146). Instead of pressing tesserae directly into their plaster bed, they are first glued upside down on a paper or canvas backing sheet, which bears the outlines of the design (or a section of it) in lateral inversion. When finished, the section is taken to the site, and its exposed side pressed into the damp plaster. Finally, the backing is peeled off to reveal the completed mosaic. Surprisingly, no one knows for certain when this indirect procedure was introduced. Very few archaeologists and art historians seem to have been at all aware of this fundamental technical problem, let alone to have approached it with sufficient knowledge of the mosaicist's practice.

In 1930 Albert Ippel used the assumption of indirect setting in classical times when he tried to explain various inconsistencies in the Alexander mosaic (*pls 19–21*): the horse which is seen from the rear has only three legs; in the centre of the picture, the bottom end of the lance which cuts across the tree is set at a slightly lower level than the rest – and there are more such points which, while not affecting the great overall impression, are noticeable and confusing enough on closer inspection of the panel. From all these Ippel concluded that sections must have been executed independently and inconsistently, and then joined incorrectly. But this might equally well have happened in the direct system, and, although the inconsistencies remain puzzling, Ippel's suggestion of shoddy workmanship conflicts so absurdly with the obvious importance and excellence of the mosaic that it is no longer given much credence. Yet, the theory that the Romans did use the indirect system can still be heard. Indeed, Klaus Parlasca has argued, with considerable acumen, that the system was 'general' in pictorial panels of the Imperial period, whereas simple patterns were set in the direct way. He feels that the operation of transferring more complicated designs to the working base would have been too difficult by the direct system; but to practising mosaicists today this is a routine procedure (see p. 146). On the other hand the question of how the Romans might have accomplished the lateral inversion of the original design which is required for indirect setting remains unsolved as long as there is no archaeological trace of Roman tracing paper, which would have

1 Wave-crest pattern

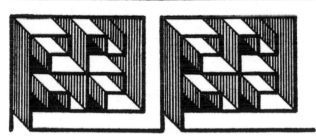

2 Double meander

3 Perspectival double meander

4 Fret border

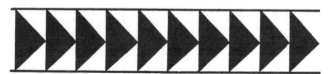

5 Triangle border

6 Cable

7 Four-strand plait border or guilloche band

8 Cable and wave patterns within a meander

CLASSICAL PAVEMENT PATTERNS I
A selection from the large number of common border
ornaments. The coiled shape of the Greek wave-crest (1)
is stylized to form the angular meander (2-3). Simple
basic elements are varied by complication (6-7), or by
combination with others (8). See also area patterns, p. 57

47

been indispensable for the operation. For direct work, of course, none was needed if the intended design was projected on a 'squared-up' working base. This was quite feasible even for the most complicated section, the *emblema*; where no tray of durable material has been found underneath, a shallow wooden box or a temporary cement base may well have been used to make the *emblema* portable. Where portions of figures reach out beyond the edge of the *emblema*, they must have been added after the portable panel had been set into the pavement, as Parlasca has shown in an Imperial period fragment from Nola (Parlasca, Pl. 102,2) in which details, such as the tail end of a snake, protrude beyond the edge of the delicate *emblema* into the coarser *tessellatum* work. But this does not necessarily imply that one portion has been produced directly and the other indirectly. In the Bacchus mosaic at Le Bardo in Tunis (Inv. A-103), for example, the delicate *vermiculatum* of the vine tendrils twining out of Bacchus's staff to surround the *emblema* has no doubt been set first, and the white background filled in later with tesserae in random order. This entanglement of the pictorial *vermiculatum* with the neighbouring areas virtually excludes the use of two different systems in this particular mosaic, and makes the use of indirect application seem highly improbable. But if this Bacchus mosaic is direct work, there is no reason why the same should not be true of all ancient *emblemata* as well.

In fact, a better case can be made out for thinking that, if the Romans did know the indirect system, they would have used it above all exactly where Parlasca feels they used the direct system: in the plainer portions. This would have helped them to industrialize their vast production of tessellated pavements, for, by laying their tesserae evenly on a table, face down, they would automatically have obtained the plane surface required in floors, and the final sanding operation would have been more than half done. However, it does not necessarily follow that this is what they did do; they may just as easily have had other labour-saving methods, such as setting the tesserae in the direct way and then, while the mortar was still malleable, laying a plank over them to knock or press them into line, ready for sanding. To sum up: there is no definite proof of, but even less proof against, the use of the indirect system in antiquity, or indeed at any time before Salviati in the nineteenth century (p. 103), and it seems, on the whole, unlikely.

V RAVENNA: the so-called Mausoleum of Galla Placidia. Detail from the *Greca* on the underside of the southern arch. 424/450. Width of detail approximately 60 cm.
The small cruciform building was intended as a tomb for the daughter of Emperor Theodosius the Great and mother of Valentinian III, in whose name she ruled the Western Empire from Ravenna. The meander ornament, in which the classical tradition remains alive in this Christian building, can be seen either as a flat or as a perspectival design – not unlike Op Art. It ranks among the most perfect achievements of the art of mosaic.

VI ROME: S. Maria Maggiore. The young Moses before Pharaoh's daughter – a scene from the Old Testament cycle in the nave. From the reign of Pope Sixtus III (432–40).
The compact figures are still marked by the dramatic movement of the classical era. Only about fifty shades of colour have been used in this cycle. The relatively small panels are mounted on solid bases, like classical *emblemata*, and were presumably completed before being installed high above the nave – which may account for the fact that they were made far too small to be seen from the floor of the basilica.

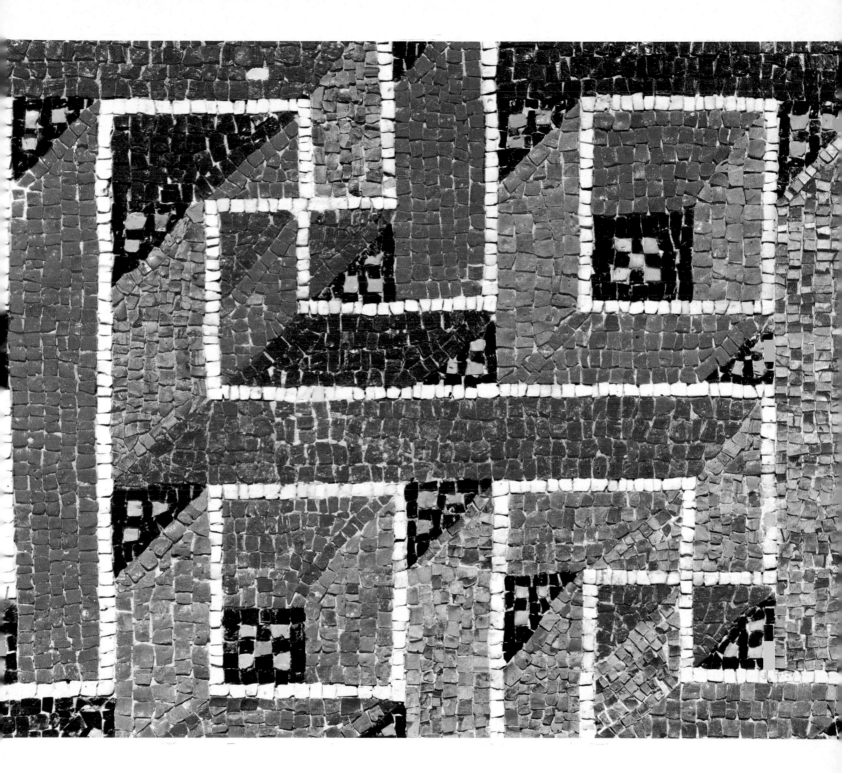

V

VI

· As *emblemata* were portable, there may have been occasions when they were used as independent pictures: Suetonius relates, somewhat bafflingly, that Caesar's campaign equipment included *tessellata et sectilia pavimenta*. These can hardly have been complete pavements for the floor of the general's tent, and were more probably small picture panels, similar to the mosaic icons of the late Middle Ages (see p. 87 and *pl. 78*).

About the same time, according to Pliny, 'paved surfaces were driven from the ground level and moved to vaulted ceilings made of glass' (*pulsa deinde ex humo pavimenta in camaras transiere vitro*). He adds that the new form of decoration would no doubt have been used in the Baths of Agrippa (21 BC) and on the ceilings of the Theatre of Scaurus (*aedile* in 58 BC), 'had it been invented earlier'. Pliny's reference to 'glass' bears witness that, even in the earliest Roman wall mosaics, smalti were used to a much larger extent than they had been in floors. He makes no mention of the wall mosaics in Pompeii which he, who was to die there in the eruption of AD 79, would have seen during earlier visits; however, in his own day they were probably no longer novel enough to be remarked upon. In fact, about forty specimens have been discovered at Pompeii and Herculaneum alone (all from the brief period 62–79), and others in Rome, Ostia, Anzio and Leptis Magna in Africa. They are still confined to small surfaces such as columns, niches, occasionally vaults (*pl. 35*) and particularly nymphaea and fountains (*pl. 23*). They are, as a rule, not found on interior walls, which could equally well be painted, but rather on exterior surfaces where they provided a weather-proof coat. Appropriately, they differ from pavements in two respects. Iconographically, they tend to draw on aquatic fauna and flora, and to substitute native Roman ornamental motifs for the traditional Greek ones. Technically, they often incorporate rows of sea-shells, and they have a polychrome sparkle, sometimes rather garish, obtained by using largely glass tesserae which are mounted at differing angles and not planed (although incorrect restoration does give that impression in some cases). These wall mosaics, and the niches in particular, are the precursors of the vaults of Christian churches. The historian Flavius Vopiscus, writing in the early fourth century, mentions a wealthy citizen who had his house decorated with glass cubes, so this was apparently still unusual even at that time. As yet, mosaic had conquered walls only in a limited way.

Roman Black-and-white Style

Black-and-white pavements were, both numerically and aesthetically, a more important Roman achievement than wall mosaics, although their introduction in the first century BC arose largely from reasons of economy. Classical mosaic, unlike its Byzantine successor, was not primarily religious, even though some of its mythological representations may well have been occasioned by apotropaic or other superstitious motives. The images of gods and goddesses were used to decorate private residences, public baths and other utilitarian edifices, and the secular purposes of the buildings were reflected in the lively and catholic variety of subject matter of their mosaics. This ranged from history and legend to drama and sports, from still-lifes and landscapes to hunting and agriculture. Mosaic had become so popular as a floor-covering that there was a need for a less expensive type, and the solution adopted was to cut the polychrome multiplicity of tesserae down to black (basalt) and white (marble or limestone). This was evidently regarded as a substitute, as is suggested, for example, by a floor near the Porta Romana in the harbour town of Ostia, in which damage to a seven-colour pattern has been repaired in coarser black-and-white only – obviously to save money. But it is at Ostia that black-and-white mosaic as a distinctive style can be studied at its best. The tessellated pavements outside the shipping-agents' offices in the so-called 'Piazza delle Corporazioni', with their marine motifs such as ships, fishes and exotic animals, were clearly serving much the same commercial purpose as graphic art in modern advertising. Financial economy engendered aesthetic economy – a sparse style that distils the quintessence of the medium.

The black-and-white style is, of course, more limited – or rather, more disciplined – in its means of expression. It observes the functional nature of mosaic as a surface decoration and makes no attempt to create an impression of spatial depth and background. Yet it does not confine itself to flat profile but uses the graphic means of internal white lines in a simple and powerful manner (not unlike that of lino-cut) to render modelled volume and quite complicated convolutions of figures (pl. 27). Its terse strength shows the stamp of Rome, no longer that of Greece.

In Italy black-and-white figure work predominated until the third century, but seems to have been little used in the provinces – though there is a British example in the two sea-horses set in an otherwise four-colour pavement of the middle of the second century in the Roman villa at Fishbourne, near Chichester. It is akin to the ancient style of Olynthos, but here are two points of difference: the cut cubes of the Romans permit greater precision and sharper contrasts than round natural pebbles, and secondly, the black ground that had been typical of Greek mosaic has given way to the white ground which was to remain prevalent throughout the Roman era (in polychrome as well as black-and-white compositions). Playing with black and white also encouraged ambiguities of perspective and other optical effects in abstract patterns which prefigure Op Art (pl. 24, figs 3 and 11 on pp 47 and 57). Similar effects were also explored in polychrome mosaic (pl. V).

Another, and far-reaching, result of the tendency to simplify technique and style was the return to the practice of using the same type of material for both the principal images and the surrounding ornament. Superfine detail in minute tesserae was abandoned and, with it, the *emblema* – at least in the literal sense of a separately produced insert panel – although the principle of arranging a floor layout around a centre-piece was never to disappear altogether. The separation of *opus tessellatum* and *opus vermiculatum*, which had basically been an artificial one, gave way to a new technical and artistic fusion for which modern archaeology has coined the term *opus musivum*. Figures were no longer restricted to the narrow confines of an *emblema*, but were able to reach out, to become larger and to expand over the entire floor. It was this freer type of composition which spread far and wide during the luxuriant florescence of mosaic in the latter part of the Imperial era.

The paved roads of the Roman legions had paved the way for the spread of sophisticated pavements over the Empire, from Spain to the Caucasus, from Asia Minor to North Africa. Even in the remote province of Britain no less than six hundred classical mosaics have so far been unearthed, two thirds of them in villas rather than on urban sites. Apart from imported material, local types of stone were used in the provinces, and there is even evidence of local production of glass tesserae in furnaces, such as the one found at Trier in Germany. A few particularly fine *emblemata* may have been shipped from Mediterranean studios but, as a rule, the construction of pavements seems to have been carried out on the spot by Greek master mosaicists, or at least under their direction. Local artisans were also trained, though they did not always attain their tutors' perfection in either technique or design, and in some pavements – at Fishbourne for example – the provincial origin can be very obvious. Nevertheless, workshops were clearly equipped with standard designs and pattern books which ensured sound quality and a measure of stylistic uniformity throughout the Empire, particularly in geometric ornament. This made it possible for a colonial territory such as Germany to produce work as superb as the great Dionysos mosaic on the floor of a banqueting hall discovered next to Cologne Cathedral: an elegant fugue composed of stone and smalti. Squares, with other squares diagonally superimposed, form eight-pointed stars with lozenges between them, framing thirty-one pictorial panels of various shapes representing scenes from the Dionysos myth (*pls 14–15*), or depicting fish, fowl and fruit as a foretaste of the sumptuous meal awaiting the guests. The soft, allusive lyricism of the figures of the Cologne pavement – almost like watercolour – helps to support a dating around AD 220, which would make it contemporary with certain scenes from Antioch (*pl. 30*). This masterly impressionism, already suggested at Pompeii, is a form of the expressionistic quality of mosaic – if both terms are understood as describing, not phases in the recent history of art, but aesthetic principles opposed to illusionism. It is a style which does not seek to imitate either nature or painting but, by juxtaposing dabs of different colours to let them blend and create a unified impression in the eye, makes logical use of the essential fact that mosaic consists of individual particles.

By this time the tesserae of the white background were often laid in a fan pattern (as can be seen in the Cologne mosaic) – an arrangement characteristic of some of the pavements in the Great Palace at Byzantium which can be dated three hundred years later. This is just one example of the features, common to different countries and centuries, which can so often bedevil the task of assigning a mosaic to its correct date and place. There were numerous styles and trends in the provinces, not all of them following similar courses, for mosaic in this period was as lively as never before, and possibly as never since. In view of such an embarrassment of riches, this survey can do no more than hint at some of the more important aspects, and leave it to a small selection of pictures to tell their own vivid story.

The dry soil of North Africa has preserved a particularly impressive number of Roman tessellated floors. A mere fraction of the thousands found in the fertile coastal strip, stretching south from Carthage, has been sufficient to make Tunisia's little-known National Museum at Le Bardo by far the world's richest treasure-house of ancient mosaics, surpassing many times in quantity as well as rivalling in quality the great collections in Rome and Naples. While it is true that these provincial artists lacked the aesthetic discipline of the Greeks, some of their formal components are not as naïve as they may seem when combined with classical imagery. Afro-oriental cultural sub-strata are recognizable in such conventions as the little wavy lines symbolizing water, which bring the Egyptian hieroglyph for *n* to mind (*pls 28–9*). Egyptian and Assyrian traditions of mural painting and relief may well be behind the frequent arrangement of images in horizontal rows or 'registers' (*pl. II*) – a device which is also found in Trajan's Column in Rome and in the Bible stories adorning the walls of churches (e. g. *pl. 61*). Narrative urges are stronger than decorative ones. The first and finest features of the African school are an affectionate realism in the treatment of figures (*pl. 28–9*), vigorous vitality, and a sensuous love of colour, both in terms of subject matter and of technique.

No wonder that mosaicists from Africa were apparently brought over to Sicily by a patron with a zest for life – possibly the Emperor Maximianus Herculius (d. 310) – to adorn his stately hunting lodge near the modern hill-town of Piazza Armerina with mosaic pavements in almost all its forty-six rooms, from the great hall to the servants' latrine. The sprawling hunting scenes (*pl. I*); the pictures of circus contests, fishing and the vintage, not forgetting the girl athletes (of slightly later date) displaying their skills and their charms in prototype bikinis (*pl. II*) – all this teeming wealth of figures makes the Piazza Armerina villa what must be the liveliest picture-book of Roman life we have; and besides all this there are grand mythological compositions, as well as geometric designs exemplifying most of the well-known patterns. These pavements, totalling 38,000 square feet and all dating from the same period, amount to a gallery summarizing in a great retrospective the principal features of Roman mosaic art at a moment in history when, under Maximianus's victorious opponent, Constantine, Christianity was poised to transform the ancient world.

An even wider, but less homogeneous, cross-section has survived at Antioch, though it can no longer be studied *in situ*. Hardly a single better-class house in this Eastern metropolis seems to have been without tessellated floors, and the styles represented span half a millennium, from the early Imperial era to the earthquake that destroyed the city in 526. In this centre of Hellenistic civilization there was a predilection for the classic panel division rather than free-ranging compositions like those of Africa. Borders surrounding the pavement became more luxuriant and contained more figures. At the same time, stylizing tendencies made themselves felt, such as the pointillistic combination of tesserae in different colours (*pl. 30*), or the calculated distortion of figures to counterbalance the perspectival foreshortening of features more removed from the eye – trends which already heralded the expressionism of Byzantine mosaic murals.

Abstract designs from the classical canon enabled even Jews to enjoy mosaic decoration without violating the religious law against graven images of animate creatures. Herod had such designs in his hill fortress at Masada, and Roman braiding patterns were to persist in Syria and Palestine until well into the Islamic period, as in the pavements of the Ummayyad palace at Khirbet el-Minya which date from the eighth century – a time when very different Byzantine-Islamic ceilings were already being executed in Jerusalem and Damascus (*pl. 75*). Yet not everyone was strict about keeping the Second Commandment: there were

9 Quatrefoil formed by intersecting circles

10 Lozenges forming eight-pointed stars, squares with cable knots and fret borders, triangles and a cable border

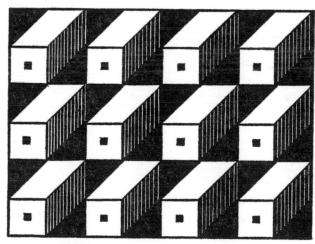

11 Squares and lozenges giving the perspective effect of square beams

12 Cable knots in *pelta* crosses (*pelta*: a shield with crescent-shaped cross-section, changed to an S curve in *pelta* crosses)

13 Alternating triangles in hour-glass formation

CLASSICAL PAVEMENT PATTERNS II
Area patterns, like ornamental borders (p. 47), are
variations and elaborations of simple geometrical motifs

even synagogues and churches in which plants, animals and human beings were briskly pictured, basically in the classical tradition, which remained alive for centuries, but with a liveliness and liberty akin to that of Africa. The pavements in the church of the Multiplication of Loaves and Fishes by the Sea of Galilee (fourth or fifth century) seem to be unaware of the religious character of the building in their gay display of brightly-coloured animals and flowers. However, the groups of figures are placed in awkward isolation on the white ground, the handling is flat and there is an emphasis on contours which is so often a sign of weakness in mosaic art, suggesting the hand of an artist not competent enough to give shape to his designs by means of colour alone. In the Beth-Alpha Synagogue at Hefziba (early seventh century) this has reached a stage where the clumsily shaped figures are indicated by little more than their empty outlines. This is not a case of sophisticated simplification, as it had been in the Roman black-and-white style. It is a coarsening which betrays decline.

But decline was not universal. In the centres of power of late antiquity, the art of classical mosaic rose once more to produce some of its finest achievements. Among these must be counted the pavement of the Great Palace of Byzantium. Its date is very uncertain – probably around 500 – but there is no doubt that in both imagery and style it still belongs to the classical tradition, although in the forceful lines in which the tesserae of the figures are set, a stylization which is 'Byzantine' in the normal sense of the word is already emerging.

S. Costanza: Peak and Watershed

There is no neat break between classical Roman and medieval Christian mosaic. The change of direction was evolutionary rather than revolutionary, despite the change of religion. But if a watershed has to be identified, it is the barrel vaulting of the circular colonnade in the church of S. Costanza in Rome (*pl. IV*). The ambiguity of this rotunda is illustrated by the fact that the Renaissance took it to be a temple of Bacchus; whereas it had almost certainly been built either as a baptistry or as a mausoleum for the Christian Emperor Constantine's daughter Constantina (not his sister Constantia as its modern name seems to imply) – presumably before her death in 354. There is Christian imagery in the two mosaics of the lateral apses (of slightly later date and somewhat cruder design), and there may also have been a Christian meaning in the dome mosaic, dismantled in 1620 and known only from drawings. The arcade mosaic is certainly the earliest vault mosaic *within* a Christian building and is paralleled only in the fragmentary dome of the mausoleum of Centcelles, near Tarragona (353/358, *pl. 36*). At the same time, and above all, S. Costanza is clearly Roman – the finest, the largest and the best-preserved Roman vault mosaic. The ground – white, as in Roman pavements – is composed of marble tesserae, while smalti are used for figures and ornament. Most of the sections of the vault are divided into circular or rhombic panels, again in the manner of Roman floors; in others many-coloured birds and plants and jugs are scattered as on an ἀσάρωτος οἶκος, pigeons are perched on the rim of a bowl like those of Sosos of Pergamon, vintaging *putti* scamper among the branches like those at Piazza Armerina – all clearly in pagan homage to Dionysos, blissfully unconcerned about Christian attempts to interpret these scenes as representing the Lord's Vineyard, or even the Last Judgment (after Revelation XIV 17–20). The reason for the supreme excellence of these mosaics is that they are something more than splendid decoration. From the austere pattern above the entrance a cyclic progression leads through all the sections of the arcade vault to the site of the sarcophagus in ever-increasing liveliness and magnificence, which is finally heightened, but not transcendentalized, by the triumphant glow of gold smalti. S. Costanza is the radiant finale to the sensuousness of late antiquity and a glorious prelude to a thousand years in which mosaic was to serve the Church as the noblest of medieval arts.

34 AQUILEIA: South Basilica. Jonah being thrown to the whale. AD 310/320. Dimensions of detail approximately 125 x 100 cm.
Detail from a large Roman pavement in rather provincial style with some Christian (and so-called 'crypto-Christian') images.

35 ROME: Necropolis below St Peter's. Vault mosaic depicting Christus-Sol in his chariot (detail). Third century AD. Height of detail about 70 cm.
Smalti and stone. Bright yellow ground, green vine tendrils, some gold tesserae.

36 CENTCELLES, near Tarragona: Mausoleum. Young Vintager. Probably 353/358.
The earliest surviving Christian dome mosaic and contemporary with the vaults of S. Costanza in Rome (pl. IV), where the dome mosaic is no longer extant. This fragmentary mosaic is mainly classical in inspiration, but contains some Christian motifs. The mausoleum is possibly that of Emperor Constans I, who was assassinated in the Pyrenees in 350.

37 TABARKA, Tunisia. Christian tomb with mosaic incrustation. Fourth century, Length about 2 m. Musée National du Bardo, Tunis.
This application of mosaic is only known from Christian Africa.

38 ROME: S. Maria Maggiore, nave. The Israelites crossing the Red Sea (detail). Probably 432/440.

39 ROME: S. Giovanni in Laterano, Baptistry. Scrolls in the apse. Fifth century.
The illustrations on this page exemplify the conservative nature of mosaic art. Certain motifs, some of them of classical origin (cf. pl. 33), are repeated for many centuries with very little change.

40 JERUSALEM: Qubbat aṣ-Ṣakhra (Dome of the Rock Mosque). Scrolls in the dome. c. 700.

41 ROME: S. Clemente. Scrolls in the apse. c. 1125.

42 RAVENNA: S. Vitale, presbytery. Empress Theodora and her entourage. 526/547. 270 x 410 cm.
Mother-of-pearl discs used for jewellery. Gold background.

43 RAVENNA: the so-called Mausoleum of Galla Placidia. Pigeons drinking (detail). 424/450. Width of detail about 80 cm.
Blue background. (See also notes to pls V and 7.)

44 PALERMO: Royal Palace of the Normans, the so-called Room of King Roger. Detail from the vault mosaic. Probably 1160/70 (i. e. the reign of William I rather than Roger II).
The Islamic influence at work in Sicily is seen, for instance, in the decorative treatment of trees. This is one of only two non-religious mosaics of the Middle Ages (the other being in the royal villa 'La Zisa' on the outskirts of Palermo), which explains the humourous mood.

45 RAVENNA: Orthodox Baptistry (of Bishop Neon). The Baptism of Christ. 450/475. Diameter about 300 cm.
Circular medallion in the centre of the dome. Its gold ground contrasts with the blue ground of the surrounding band depicting the apostles, who are dressed in gold. The way in which the Saviour's legs are made visible through the water is a technical tour de force never again equalled by other representations of the baptism — not even by the closely related scene in the Baptistry of the Arians (c. 500), also in Ravenna.

46 RAVENNA: S. Apollinare Nuovo, nave. Procession of the Martyrs. c. 561 (latest portion of the church's mosaic decoration, possibly replacing an earlier frieze in the spirit of the Arian faith). Smalti and some marble. Height 280 cm., total length of frieze 34.5 m. Opposite these sixteen figures, on the other side of the nave, sixteen holy virgins are shown in similar movement towards the sanctuary. The mosaic of the apse, no doubt originally the focal point of the decoration, has disappeared, and its absence is emphasized today by a plain plastered surface. But the architecture and the mosaic decoration were obviously designed as an integral entity to serve the liturgical purpose.

47 RAVENNA: S. Apollinare in Classe (consecrated 549). View of the nave (width about 14.25 m.).
In the centre of the apse St Apollinaris is seen standing on an unusual grassy green ground sprinkled with gold tesserae as if with sunlight. The long, spacious nave is embraced and dominated by the particularly harmonious curvature of the apse and its triumphal arch. The upper mosaic decorations date from the seventh or ninth century, the two lowest panels from the twelfth.

34

35

36

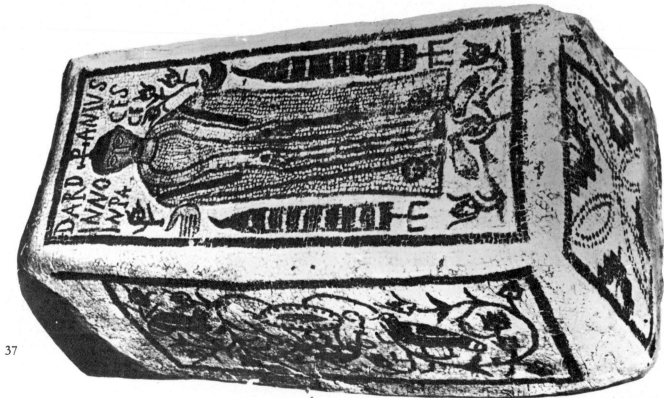

37

38

39 40

41

SVPRA SCRIPTI. REQVIE SCVNT. CORPORE

42

43

44

45

46

Second Phase: Medieval Murals

The Christian Middle Ages are regarded as the Golden Age of mosaic. This is quite literally correct, for the holy images are sumptuously set on vast backgrounds of tesserae coated with real gold, which reflect and reinforce the glory of sacred and secular majesty. The Church and the Emperor chose mosaic as their foremost didactic instrument, providing it with all the opportunities and resources that power has ever offered to art, and its supreme position was equalled by its supreme aesthetic achievement. That is not to say that mosaic in this second great phase of its history is superior to that of the classical phase. It is different, very different, not only because of its religious content, but also in function, application, format, style, technique and material. It is almost a different medium.

The fact that the very beginnings of medieval mosaic, in the early Christian buildings of Rome and Ravenna, produced some of the finest achievements of the medium indicates that it had not, of course, been instantly created by the spirit of the victorious religion but had adopted and adapted the traditions of the pagan past. At first, classical styles and forms were used unchanged and made to serve the new God. In the basilica at Aquileia, unmistakably Roman pavements of the fourth century show birds, deer and rams as well as the Good Shepherd and the story of Jonah (*pl. 34*). In the contemporary Romano-British pavement from Hinton St Mary in Dorset (now in the British Museum) Bellerophon and the Chimera happily coexist with the XP monogram of the Saviour. Christian symbols, but trodden underfoot: here is one obvious reason why the Christian religion could not be very interested in floor mosaics. In 427 the *Codex Theodosianus* forbade the use of sacred symbols in pavements in the Eastern Empire.

But early Christianity had already taken up the promising idea of mural and vault mosaic. The scale was small at first – as in the third-century mosaic vault in the necropolis below St Peter's (*pl. 35*), a remarkable document of transition which, against a brilliant yellow ground, shows Christ in the posture of the Sun God riding on his chariot, his face framed by a halo in which gold tesserae have been used. It is likely that more extensive mosaic decorations adorned the great churches of Constantine's era, none of which have survived. African fellow-Christians of St Augustine's in the fourth and fifth centuries covered box-shaped tombs with a coat of mosaic featuring a portrait of the deceased and various religious symbols and inscriptions – an unusual application for a medium which is not normally used as a skin for three-dimensional forms (*pl. 37*). In the middle of the fourth century, designs from pagan pavements appeared on the barrel vaulting of S. Costanza (*pl. IV*), and in the same period the dome of the mausoleum at Centcelles in Spain was decorated with both profane and biblical scenes (*pl. 36*). The rise of the large mosaic from floor to ceiling was complete.

Significantly, both S. Costanza and Centcelles are royal as well as religious edifices. In classical times, the vast majority of tessellated pavements had been commissioned by private patrons; in the Middle Ages, mosaicists worked for suprapersonal authorities able to spend considerably greater sums, and this fact helped to extend the scope and size of mosaic work so much that a change occurred in its very nature. It now had to cover vast expanses of wall and vault, and the complex articulation of the architectural surfaces inevitably transformed the articulation of the mosaic decoration into a problem more complex than it had been in the era of simple rectangular floors. Another important factor was that its purpose was no longer decoration for its own sake, but its calculated psychological effect on the community: propaganda for the faith. This aim conditioned the mode of presentation. The primary intention was no longer to depict the world as it was but to depict the suprapersonal patrons as they wished to be seen – no longer mere representation but idealization – and this was something which mosaic, with its stylizing qualities, was eminently suited to achieve. The lengthy process of working with an intractable material tends to act as a filter, dematerializing and depersonalizing both the impression of reality and the inspiration of the artist and creating a distance and detachment between the natural object and the work of art on the one hand, and between the work of art and its beholder on the other. These were some of the forces that formed the style of medieval mosaic, and, as a result of the pre-eminence among the arts which mosaic enjoyed during this long period, its characteristics had a far-reaching influence on the characteristics of the Byzantine style in other arts as well.

The cumbersome technique of mosaic encourages a rather conservative approach which coincides with the conservative nature of institutionalized religion. At this period it had to reflect the firmly established philosophical and political order of medieval Christendom which rivals the homogeneous permanence of the equally hierarchical civilizations of Egypt and China, and the result was similar: a strong artistic continuity, spanning more than a thousand years and giving rise to an almost monotonous uniformity of recurring motifs. As in Egypt, this was reinforced by an archaizing tendency, an inclination not only to continue the styles of the immediate past but to revive those of more distant periods. The classical scrolls in the apse of S. Clemente in Rome (*pl. 41*), which date from about 1125, confusingly resemble those in S. Maria Maggiore – which were not produced until around 1290, but are probably a remade version of the original scrolls of about 435 – which are closely related to the fifth-century ones in the Lateran Baptistry (*pl. 39*); the same features are found in the Dome of the Rock Mosque in Jerusalem dating from 691/92 (*pl. 40*). It also has to be remembered that most churches, unlike ancient pavements, have not lain buried under the soil but have been in constant use for centuries, and that this has made repairs and alterations necessary which have often obscured the original styles and dates. For instance, the much-admired apse of S. Pudenziana in Rome, showing Christ in Majesty, dates from around 400 but has gradually been turned into a *Kitsch* copy of the original and looks like a bastardized nineteenth-century re-working of a rather pedestrian Renaissance mural. Hurried tourists can hardly be blamed for not noticing much difference between mosaics of this kind and certain archaizing church decorations of the nineteenth and twentieth centuries.

There is, however, one other factor which unites the mosaics of the long medieval period, and distinguishes them from those of classical antiquity: the material with its consequences in terms of technique and style. If hard-wearing natural stone had been ideal for pavements, the walls and vaults of the Middle Ages were able to take advantage of the more fragile glass smalti with their greater variety of colours. At the start of the Christian period, as in the biblical panels above the nave of S. Maria Maggiore (*pl. VI*), barely fifty shades were used. Nonetheless, by juxtaposing them boldly, mosaicists were able to obtain expressionistic and constructivistic effects like those of the stupendous *Greca* in the mausoleum of Galla Placidia in Ravenna (*pl. V*), or the coloured clouds surrounding the gold-clad Saviour in SS. Cosma e Damiano in Rome (*pl. VII*). They also broke up colour areas in pointillistic fashion, by juxtaposing tesserae of graded tones, or even of contrasting colours, to give sparkle to an otherwise flat patch and obtain from a limited palette the effect of various intermediate shades (*pls VI, VII*). Besides its colour, the outstanding qualities of glass mosaic are, of course, its luminosity and its ability to reflect light. Since walls and vaults, unlike floors, do not have to be smooth, it now became possible to make conscious use of these properties, and of the insular autonomy of each tessera, to engender one of mosaic's most distinctive means of expression. This is the method whereby each tessera is set at an individual angle, so that it catches and reflects light in a way calculated by the mosaicist, making the faceted surface glisten and glimmer like the starry sky (see p. 146 and *fig. 15* on p. 142).

Mosaic design was also influenced by the fact that church murals are usually seen from a distance. The experienced artist knew that he had to counterbalance foreshortening in the upper reaches of walls, or overcome the even more complex perspectival distortions caused by the curves of vaults and apses. He also had to appreciate that fine detail would hardly be distinguishable, so that simplification was even more desirable than in the case of floors. This last problem was not recognized at first and, even in later periods, was not always taken into account. The small biblical panels in S. Maria Maggiore (*pls VI, 38*), dating from the fourth or fifth centuries and still showing Roman vigour in the liveliness of their figures and their dramatic compositions, are masterpieces; but their excellence is quite literally misplaced, for, high above the nave of this big basilica, they can hardly be noticed, let alone studied, by worshippers below. Presumably it was just poor planning that placed them at such remote height, condemning them to a magnificent futility from which they were freed only by the modern camera; yet, for us, there is a sense of medieval mysticism in the thought that pious artists spent years of patient labour composing this hallelujah in colour for no other eyes but those of the Creator.

Liturgical Function

Increasingly, however, the decoration was conditioned by the conscious intention of promoting the faith. The lines of intellectual and stylistic development traced so perceptively by Otto Demus in his succinct and brilliant book *Byzantine Mosaic Decoration* can only be suggested here. Originally, Christian mosaic decoration was nothing more than an embellishment, a secondary feature conceived after the building itself and fitted into bare-looking places as an essentially independent element, without really being related to the architectural context. Floral patterns can be applied anywhere without necessarily attaining an architectural and a liturgical function. Even a religious composition such as the Heavenly Jerusalem in S. Pudenziana (*c.* 400), where the representation of a long roof cuts across the conch, shows little regard for the shape of the apse. Instances of more sensitive apsidal design are found in SS. Cosma e Damiano (*c.* 530, detail on *pl. VII*) and, from a later period, at Torcello, Cefalù and Monreale (*pls 57, 62, 65*). From an early date the domes of rotundas, in particular, invited an articulated layout which echoed the centralized scheme of classical *emblema* floors. In the fourth and fifth centuries, the undersides of the domes of S. Costanza, Centcelles, the Orthodox Baptistry at Ravenna and the baptistry adjoining Naples Cathedral were all divided up into horizontal circular bands and vertical segments, while the niches below them were emphasized as separate architectural features. It was realized that the architectural mass and its skin had to be treated as one entity, and that decoration could play its part in shaping and pervading architectural space so that both could unite to serve the liturgical purpose. In Byzantine churches of the Middle Ages, with their ascending domes and undulating vaults, this unity of mosaic with architecture has been ideally achieved.

Mural mosaic should, like the structure of the building, project itself into the space which it encloses and upon the people in that space, and this principle contributes to the tendency to show figures in a frontal posture. Facing the spectator, they often stand detached from one another, devoid of any narrative or even compositional relationship, frequently perched on the bottom border of the picture area. Occasionally they push a foot beyond the edge, as if to step out from the wall into the space, approach the faithful and take part in their worship. The hieratic 'Byzantine' posture, which is emphasized by the stylizing tendency of mosaic technique, moves the iconic figure closer to men while at the same time removing it into the dimension of majesty.

Among the most magnificent instances of this are the panels representing Emperor Justinian and Empress Thedora and their entourages in the church of S. Vitale in Ravenna, which was consecrated in 547 or 548 (*pl. 42*). They are examples of transition. They are framed panels, but are placed in an architectural

VII ROME: SS. Cosma e Damiano. Apse mosaic. 526/530.
The majestic figure of Christ in this church which stands on the Forum combines something of the realistic posture of the classical era with the stylized drapery typical of the Byzantine epoch. The clouds are rendered in bold expressionistic colours.

VIII ROME: S. Prassede, Cappella di S. Zenone. Vault mosaic. 817/824.
The little chapel, with its almost oriental sparkle, is the jewel among the products of the brief period of intense activity in the field of mosaic under Pope Paschal I. The four angels closely resemble those in the Archbishop's Chapel in Ravenna (*c.* 500) as well as those in the lateral chapel of Torcello Cathedral (twelfth century).

relationship to one another on opposite walls; the men and women are linked together as members of their respective groups, but all stare ahead into space, and, while some of the faces are vivid portraits, those of the lower court echelons are stereotyped masks; the robes are individualized, but subordinated, by means of the concerted flow of their draperies, to a compositional idea which gives prominence to the illustrious central figure, whose splendour is enriched by the use of large mother-of-pearl discs in the diadem and other jewellery. The emergence of the Byzantine style, which these panels show at an early stage, can be studied, as though in a display case, in the small city of Ravenna – a cultural cross-roads which has been the capital of West Roman emperors, Gothic kings and the Byzantine provincial governor.

A monument from the West Roman period in Ravenna is the so-called mauso-leum of Galla Placidia (d. 450), an emperor's daughter who became regent of the Empire. It is close in date and style to the Naples baptistry and, in the Eastern empire, to the church of Hagios Georgios at Salonika (*pl. 52*). The figures are still Roman in their realistic movement, but they are placed against the dark blue background which is characteristic of early Christian mosaic. Inheriting this blue ground from Roman niches (e. g. *pl. 22*), Christian artists had deepened it to arrive at a blueness symbolic of infinity which enveloped figures in transcendental mystery. Another effect of this spiritualizing process is evident in the drinking doves (*pl. 43*) when their stylized simplicity is com-pared with the rich illusionism of a late Greek version of this motif introduced by Sosos of Pergamon (*pl. 7*).

This tendency was soon to be reinforced by an influence leading to even stronger stylization and emanating from Byzantium which was absorbing and developing the traditions of the Persian empire, and thus the ancient Eastern concepts of idolization of royal power and the idealizing function of art. In the territory of the East Roman empire itself, few early Byzantine monuments have survived the onslaught of Islam, but their style is no doubt reflected in the Ravenna of Theodoric, King of the Ostrogoths (493–526), who had been brought up in Constantinople. Adjoining his palace he built the Basilica now called S. Apollinare Nuovo but once known as the church 'with the golden sky' (*in coelo aureo*) because of the golden mosaic background which dominated its interior. Byzantine formality and formalism are already manifest in the two early groups surround-ing the Virgin with Child and the Christ in Majesty. The figures, which show little modelling, are placed in a hieratic pose against the golden ground from which they are gazing forth. In the two long friezes of saints (not added until about 561, after the end of the Gothic kingdom) there is hardly any attempt at lively individuality, the almost identical figures in their almost identically draped gar-ments being subordinated entirely to their liturgical and architectural functions: the two processions marching towards the apse guide the eye in the direction of the altar, emphasizing the longitudinal aspect of the church. The two broad strips of wall above the nave were obviously provided with this mosaic decoration in mind, for the architecture and its decoration are complementary parts of a consistent design – although, unfortunately, the mosaics of the apse and the arch in front of it are no longer extant. But what is missing in S. Apollinare, the dominating effect of a great Ravenna apse decoration, can be seen just outside the city in the basilica of S. Apollinare in Classe, which displays the essential features of the Byzantine style and iconography (*pl. 47*).

The first period of medieval mosaic ended in an intense, if somewhat forced, Indian summer under Pope Paschal I (817–24) in Rome. In his three churches – S. Maria in Domnica, S. Prassede and S. Cecilia – there is a conscious harking back to the traditions of Ravenna and of SS. Cosma e Damiano in Rome itself (*pl. VII*). Blue grounds appear again (alongside gold ones). The apsidal composition in S. Prassede is modelled, though hardly with outstanding skill, on that of SS. Cosma e Damiano of three centuries before. The colourful East is shimmering luxuriantly in the tiny space of the 'garden of paradise', as the little Cappella di S. Zenone within the church of S. Prassede has been called (*pl. VIII*). If S. Prassede is the finest among Paschal's churches, its great importance and the impression it makes derive from the comprehensiveness of the composition and of the liturgical 'programme' displayed in the apse and on the apsidal and triumphal arches.

This cyclic iconography, which was to remain basically the same for centuries, turned the church interior into a systematic model of the Christian cosmos. The towering temples of India, too, were intended to represent the heavens, and it may be that oriental influences were at work when the tradition of Roman rotundas was extended and spiritualized in the mighty Byzantine domed basilicas. Their decoration is governed by hierarchic order. The focal point – the centre of the apse – is normally occupied by Christ as Pantocrator, shown in one of a number of standard poses: sitting on a throne, standing (*pl. VII*), or, particularly later, as a head-and-shoulders portrait (*pl. 62*). In churches dedicated to the Virgin, the same place is taken by the Madonna and Child or by the *Madonna orans*, with hands raised in prayer (*pls 57–9*). Both Christ and Mary are usually clad in blue, and flanked by apostles or other appropriate saints. Less frequently, the church's patron saint is accorded the central place himself (*pl. 47*). Supporting figures and features include the animal symbols of the four evangelists, the twelve sheep representing the apostles, the Jordan river, the walls of Bethlehem and Jerusalem and, above the central figure, the hand of God or the 'tabernacle' (tent of paradise). Alternatively, some of these motifs may appear on the triumphal arch in front of the apse, or else that space may be filled by crucial scenes from the life of Christ, such as the Nativity (*pls 48–50*). The usual position for narrative picture sequences from the Old or New Testament is above the nave, as in S. Maria Maggiore (*pls VI, 38*) and at Monreale (*pls 65–71*). Narrow surfaces such as those between windows lend themselves to images of standing saints (top of *pl. 46*), while heads of saints, enclosed in medallions, are often found among garlands on the underside of arches. From the centre of the dome, of course, a symbol or portrait of the Pantocrator looks down on the faithful (*pls 63–4*).

Byzantium and Islam

This hierarchic order was particularly manifest within the territory of the Greek Church. Development had, however, been interrupted when external wars of the Byzantines and the long-drawn-out iconoclastic controversy (724–843) severely hampered not only iconic representations but also mosaic production in general. When the Greek emperor, in 730, prohibited the use of icons, the Arab caliph had already imposed a similar ban on Christian churches in his domain in 723.

But Muhammad's interdict on depicting human beings did not prevent Islam from following the example of Christian emperors and bishops in making mosaic serve the faith of the Prophet and the glory of his successors – and this was done largely by employing Christian mosaicists. Apparently they were not all recruited from Byzantium but included natives of Syria who had developed a mosaic tradition of their own and even produced glass tesserae locally. Their achievement must be counted among the most beautiful monuments of the art of mosaic – arguably just because of the spiritual and aesthetic influence of Islam. Despite the sensuous Arabs' love of story-telling, their ascetic religion has, in the fine arts, largely managed to do without the narrative element, substituting floral or abstract ornament in which asceticism and luxuriance are splendidly, if paradoxically, joined.

How few of the iconographic scenes in our Christian churches really harmonize with the architectural lines! Here, under these ceilings full of shadows, lighted only by the gold sheen of the mosaics, all is dignity and mystery. Too reverential to represent in human shape the Divine Being whom he adores, the Muslim has merely sought to make of this sanctuary a marvellous garden.

In this lyrical passage, Marguerite van Berchem, the historian of mosaic, records the overwhelming impression of Jerusalem's Dome of the Rock Mosque (Qubbat aṣ-Ṣakhra, *pl. 75*), built by Caliph 'Abd al-Malik (685–705). Over 10,000 square feet of its interior surfaces are covered with mosaics in blue, green and gold, with a sprinkling of other colours. The acanthus scrolls are reminiscent of nearby Antioch and of the Hellenistic tradition which, possibly even reinforced by this more recent Syrian example, was to live on, five centuries later, in the Roman churches of S. Clemente and S. Giovanni in Laterano (*pls 39, 41*). There is also an echo of Persia (and even of Assyria) in the Sassanian wing motifs, which also subsequently found their way into Christian iconography. The oriental taste for repetition, for *parallelismus membrorum*, for symmetry and geometry – which has also affected Christian mosaic schemes – wove from these basic motifs serial patterns which could be adapted perfectly to any architectural requirement.

Byzantine artists called in by the next caliph, Al-Walîd (705–15), seem to have been responsible for the pictorial mosaics in the Great Mosque at Damascus which, rather surprisingly, represent classical and Eastern buildings and landscapes in a flamboyant manner recalling the Fourth Style of Pompeian wall-painting, with its grandiose architecture in illusionistic perspective, and even show painterly modelling. This decoration (plastered over and not rediscovered until around 1930) made the Damascus mosque 'the most beautiful thing Muslims possess today', as Muqaddasî wrote around 985.

In 965, at the request of Al-Ḥakam, Caliph of Córdoba, who wished to embellish his capital, Emperor Nikephoros Phokas dispatched to Spain a Greek master mosaicist as well as a cargo of smalti. The result was that the Córdoba mosque combined Byzantine technique, in which the Greek expert had presumably trained Arab artists, with floral designs which were their own Islamic contribution. There was also some mosaic work in Egypt and Mesopotamia. But Islam did not carry the main line of mosaic any further, developing instead two related techniques which were based on the ancient oriental tradition of ceramic tiles.

79

Earthenware tiles, with their flat glazing, do not reflect light as shimmeringly as smalti, and, no special effect being gained from setting them at varying angles, they are arranged to form even surfaces. A more important difference lies in the format of the tiles. Small mosaic tiles in standardized geometric shapes for making patterns evolved around 1300 in Persia, as well as in North Africa and Spain. Clay tiles of this type, called *zalîj* in Arabic and predominantly blue or turquoise in colour, developed, both technically and etymologically, into Spain's well-known *azulejos*, as seen in the Alhambra, and the tide of Islam was eventually to sweep similar small tiles as far abroad as India. Similar standardized tesserae, cut from marble, were used for a long time in Mameluke Egypt and in Syria for composing repeating geometric patterns. A virtually identical counterpart in the occident is 'Cosmati work' (*pl. 73*), a craftsmanlike variety of mosaic practised by the Cosmati family and others in Rome between the twelfth and fifteenth centuries as a colourful decoration on countless pillars, balustrades and floors, and even carried by them to Westminster Abbey in 1268–9.

All this can fairly be classified as mosaic. Not so, however, the quite different tiling technique which flourished in Persia and was introduced into India, particularly under the Mogul emperors (from 1526). In this case, earthenware pieces are specially cut to the individual shapes required by the design (*pl. 74*) – rather in the manner of the second type of Roman *opus sectile* and of Florentine *pietra dura* (p. 8).

Middle Byzantine Period

The art of mosaic reached Russia direct from Constantinople in 989, when the Grand Duke Vladimir of Kiev, who had been baptized and had married the Byzantine emperor's sister, invited Greek mosaicists to his city. Work in Sv. Sophia, which was to become their major achievement in Kiev, was begun in 1043 under Yaroslav, Vladimir's successor (*pls 53, 59, 64*). It is a superb piece of Byzantine workmanship. Muscles, such as those on the forehead of the Pantocrator in the dome, are indicated more by the *andamento*, or 'coursing', of the tesserae than by modelling in graded tones: colours are boldly juxtaposed; the design is flat and expressionistic; facial features and draperies are simplified, but not devoid of individuality (lower part of *pl. 59*). The freshness of style,

IX   CHIOS: Nea Moni. Centurion at the foot of the Cross. 1042/1056.
This little known monastic church represents one of the finest examples of the Middle Byzantine style of mosaic. Set against a gold ground are stylized yet dramatic figures in rich, flat colours with bold outlines and broad shadows.

X   ISTANBUL: Hagia Sophia, south tribune. Detail from the panel showing the Empress Irene (daughter of King Ladislaus of Hungary) and Emperor John II Comnenus flanking the Virgin with Child. 1118 or soon after. Dimensions of detail about 247 x 140 cm.
The surviving mosaics in this great metropolitan church (many of which were not rediscovered until around 1930) date from various centuries. In the figures of the donors of this panel, decorative stylization has been carried to a point where form nearly dissolves into mere outlines.

X

undimmed by the highly-skilled technique, may well be attributable to Russian artists, who, incidentally, were supported by local manufacture of smalti. But the Kiev churches remained the only ones in eastern Europe to receive Byzantine mosaics – unless one wishes to include St Vitus's Cathedral in Prague, where not the interior but the façade (1370–1) is decorated in a rough provincial manner which is nevertheless quite sensitive and impressive.

It was in this 'Middle Byzantine' period – from the ninth century, when iconoclasm ended, until the twelfth – that the Byzantine style reached its most characteristic form, and so did 'Byzantinism' in the deprecatory sense in which the term is often used today.

The surviving mosaics in the Hagia Sophia at Constantinople were not produced to a consistent plan, but at various times over several centuries, some of them as votive pictures of successive sovereigns. In the panel of Zoë, who was the consort of three emperors, the head of the latest spouse replaced that of his predecessor, at any rate at her last marriage in 1042. All that really mattered was the hierarchical and hieratic function, and Zoë's stereotyped posture recurs almost exactly in the figure of another empress, Irene (c. 1118, pl. X). The colourful ceremonial robe, set on the gold ground in what is hardly more than linear design, forms a resplendent surface decoration – but a superficial one, empty in both senses of the word. Even the portrait face, which seems almost to be stuck on like a photograph of a head cut out and set on a line-drawn body in a newspaper cartoon, is a rigid mask. Art is frozen out by splendour and virtuosity.

There is, of course, much superb work in Constantinople, for example, in the Hagia Sophia, the Deësis (Christ in Majesty, flanked by the Virgin and the Baptist, pl. 55) from the end of the twelfth century, or the magnificent early fourteenth-century decoration in the Kariye Cami (pl. 50), which in some ways recalls the Ravenna period. But the relatively small number of mosaics which have survived in the metropolis can no more than suggest the city's regal and religious radiance. Nonetheless, her radiation reflected in other parts of the Empire is dazzling enough.

Vigorous but at the same time deeply religious effects were achieved in such eleventh-century Greek churches as Hosios Lukas in Phokis, the Nea Moni (New Monastery) on Chios (pl. IX) and the church at Daphni near Eleusis (pl. 63), as well as at Kiev. Yet, the stylistic means were the same as those used in the capital: rich, flat colours on a gold ground, defined and internally articulated by thick contours. During this period and the years that followed, the stylization of details such as muscles, hair and drapery does not seek the gentle roundness of classical work, but has a sharp angularity which foreshadows the Gothic painting of the North. The influence of mosaic technique, which had helped so much in formulating the Byzantine style in general, can thus be recognized in the Gothic sphere where mosaic itself never gained a foothold during medieval times.

This close relationship is obvious in such examples as the Pantocrator in the cathedral at Cefalù (pl. 62). The Sicilian group of mosaics to which this belongs is mainly the work of Greek artists commissioned by Roger II and William II to deck out the Norman conquerors' new royal power with the golden trappings of emperors and caliphs. It may or may not be an accident that the only two profane mosaics of any note that survive from the Christian Middle Ages were both produced at the cosmopolitan court of Palermo: the gay hunting pictures decorating King Roger's Room at the palace (*pl. 44*) and those in the royal villa La Zisa on the outskirts of the city. The Saracen atmosphere of Sicily has imparted an oriental air to the exotic animals and trees, and the surrounding ornament is reminiscent of Islamic Syria.

Naturally, this is less noticeable in the Norman churches: Cefalù Cathedral (*pls 58, 62*), the glittering Palatine Chapel (*pl. 54*) and the curious little church known as La Martorana (*pl. 49*) in Palermo, and the crowning glory of the great cathedral at Monreale in which, within only ten years (around 1180), all the interior walls were covered with mosaics extending over 68,250 square feet (*pl. 65*). Disparaging comments have been made about the quality of the latter, yet, notwithstanding the somewhat muted colour, Monreale is remarkable for the popular (not to say Pop Art) liveliness of the biblical picture strips (*pls 66–71*) and above all for the consistency of its iconographic programme – all produced within one short space of time and under one architectural plan and, moreover, preserved intact. It is a rare piece of luck that the complete scheme in a major church can still be seen as it was intended by its designers.

Such unity is frequently lacking even in much smaller churches, such as the cathedral on the Venetian island of Torcello. The earliest portions of its apsidal decoration, the Apostles, dating from around 1100, are certainly Greek work, as is probably the slender and solitary Madonna above them which dominates the golden conch (*pl. 57*). But there is a jarring contrast, though not without its own sense of drama, between the solemn figure of the Virgin and the wild and crowded scenes of the Last Judgment decorating the wall at the opposite end. These were probably first executed in various stages around 1200 – and replaced by a copy in the nineteenth century (as Otto Demus has proved). Some of them have mannerist overtones (*pl. 61*). A direct line links the scenes of hell with those in the large dome of the baptistry in Florence (*pl. 60*) which inspired Giotto's frescos at Padua and, no doubt, Dante's *Inferno*.

Late Flowering and Decline

About the same time, in the thirteenth century, the branch of mosaic art in papal Rome once again put forth rich flowers as extensive renovation work was carried out in the great basilicas of S. Paolo fuori le mura (*c.* 1218, but destroyed by fire in 1823 and subsequently replaced), S. Giovanni in Laterano (from 1290) and S. Maria Maggiore (from 1294), as well as additions to S. Maria in Trastevere (from 1295). The marks of autumnal effort are manifest in the principal work of the period, the over-ornate apse of S. Maria Maggiore. This is crowded with modelled figures and scrolls without due feeling for articulation and architecture, and the fine detail, despite its high quality, only tends to be confusing at such great height. Names of artists appear here, the first since antiquity: Jacobus Torriti (described in an inscription as *pictor*, i. e. the designer), Philippus Rusuti, Gaddo Gaddi, and others.

In 1301, Cimabue was put in charge of mosaic decoration in Pisa Cathedral, and at least the head of St John the Evangelist in the apse seems to be his work. At St Peter's in Rome his great pupil, Giotto, may also have had a hand in the execution of his 'Navicella' mosaic (1298), showing Christ walking on the water ('*cosa meravigliosa*', according to Vasari, who would hardly have had so much admiration for the distorted version seen today). Later, Ghirlandaio designed mosaics for Florence Cathedral, and Titian, Tintoretto, Veronese and Lotto were among the cartoon painters of St Mark's in Venice, which, through the work of innumerable hands from about the twelfth until well into the nineteenth century, has become the 'Golden Basilica' – and an overwhelming hotchpotch of various styles in varying quality (*pls 76–7*).

The last master who both designed and executed his mosaics may well have been Muziano da Brescia (1528–92) who was active in St Peter's in Rome from 1576. The age of the painters had brought with it the age of the imitation of nature. Oil and fresco painting took over the predominance that mosaic had held for a thousand years, and the aesthetics and techniques of painting, as well as the personalities of painters, dominated and determined the art of mosaic itself during its long dying phase. Ghirlandaio's telling phrase that mosaic was '*pittura per l'eternità*' became reality.

Miniature Mosaics

The confusion of mosaic with painting also begot a curious, though impressive, phenomenon: Byzantine miniature mosaics (*pl. 78*). These are now rare objects, preserved only in museums and the treasuries of monasteries, but from about the eleventh to the fourteenth centuries they seem to have been very popular, being used particularly as icons, but also for such practical purposes as book covers, like the pair in the cathedral museum at Florence. On a wax base, tiny tesserae of gold, lapis lazuli and other stones and materials, possibly including glass, were assembled to form miniature pictures in the style of contemporary mosaic murals – except, of course, that such pin-head tesserae tended to resist broad stylization. Many of these portable mosaics are exquisite works of art, though this is not so much because of as in spite of the fact that they are mosaics; in the case of larger ones, such as the life-size head of Christ now in the Bargello, a stronger mosaic effect would have been obtained by using larger tesserae, or a stronger painterly effect by using paint and brush. In fact these miniatures represent effort misspent, or so it seems to us today, but for patient monks, working away on them for years, they must have been a deeply satisfying equivalent of modern hobby-lovers' matchstick models of Westminster Abbey.

As art gave way to artifice, the brilliant light of medieval Christian mosaic slowly flickered out.

48 ROME: S. Maria Maggiore. The Nativity. *c.* 1300. From the Life of the Virgin series between the windows of the apse. Designed by Jacopo Torriti.

49 PALERMO: La Martorana (S. Maria dell'Ammiraglio), spandrel in the crossing. The Nativity. 1143/1151.

50 ISTANBUL: Kariye Cami (Church of the Saviour, Chora Monastery), exonarthex. The Nativity. *c.* 1315.

51 ROME: Vatican Grottos. Head of St Peter. Probably fifth century.
Perhaps from the original church of St Peter's.

52 SALONIKA: Hagios Georgios. Head of a saint in the dome mosaic. *c.* 400, according to H. P. L'Orange.

53 KIEV: Sv. Sofia, wall of the apse. St John Chrysostom. Probably 1043/1046. Height of whole figure 2.3 m.

54 PALERMO: Palatine Chapel, north wall of northern transept. St John Chrysostom. *c.* 1150.

55 ISTANBUL: Hagia Sophia, south tribune. St John the Baptist (detail from the *Deësis*, or representation of Christ flanked by the Virgin and the Baptist). *c.* 1200, discovered 1933.

56 ROME: Vatican Grottos. St Bernard. Late fourteenth or early fifteenth century.
From the dismantled original church of St Peter's.

57 TORCELLO, near Venice: Cathedral. Virgin with Child in the apse. Twelfth century.
The blue-clad figure stands alone on the plain gold ground covering the whole conch (width about 9 m.).

58 CEFALÙ, Sicily: Cathedral. *Madonna orans* (in prayer) in the apse. 1148 or soon after.

59 KIEV: Sv. Sofia, conch of the central apse. *Madonna orans*. 1043/1046. Height of figure about 5 m.

60 FLORENCE: Baptistry of S. Giovanni. Scene of Hell from the biblical cycle in the dome. First half of the thirteenth century.

61 TORCELLO, near Venice: Cathedral. Scene of Hell in the *Last Judgment* on the wall facing the apse (*pl. 57*). The images are arranged in five horizontal 'registers'. Originally late twelfth or early thirteenth century, but completely replaced in the nineteenth.

62 CEFALÙ, Sicily: Cathedral. Pantocrator in the conch (above *Madonna orans, pl. 58*). 1148 or soon after. The apse is only about 10 m. wide, but its majesty is increased by its height. The drapery is picked out in gold and the treatment shows bold stylization. The shape of the head-and-shoulders portrait is related to that of other Pantocrator portraits in circular medallions (cf. *pls 63–4*).

63 DAPHNI, near Athens: Church of the Dormition. Pantocrator medallion in the dome. *c.* 1100.

64 KIEV: Sv. Sofia. Pantocrator medallion in the dome. 1043/1046. Diameter about 5 m.

65 MONREALE, near Palermo: Cathedral. View of the interior, a complete mosaic 'programme' (covering 6,340 sq. m.) executed by Greeks soon after 1180. Gold ground, with figures and scenes in relatively subdued colours.

66–71 MONREALE, near Palermo: Cathedral. The days of the Creation from the Old Testament cycle in the nave. Soon after 1180.
The fact that the posture of the Creator remains virtually constant from one scene to the next suggests the use of one basic cartoon. Simple but expert technique of setting.

72 CÓRDOBA: Mosque. Dome above the *mihrâb* (prayer niche). Commenced 965.
Executed under Greek direction, using few, but rich, colours (blue, red and green on a gold ground) and very small tesserae.

73 SESSA AURUNCA, Campania: Cathedral of S. Pietro, pulpit. Cosmati mosaic: geometric ornaments composed of standardized units. Second half of the thirteenth century.

74 AGRA, India. Chîni-kâ-Rauza – the supposed mausoleum of the poet Afzal Khan (d. 1639). Period of the Islamic Mogul emperors.
Glazed tiles (*chînâ* – hence the name of the building, meaning 'tomb with tiles') are used in pieces precut to the shapes required. The technique is therefore not mosaic proper, but is similar to classical *opus sectile* and Florentine *pietra dura* (see p. 8).

75 JERUSALEM: Qubbat aṣ-Ṣakhra (Dome of the Rock Mosque), dome. *c.* 700.
The principal colours are blue, green and gold.

76 VENICE: S. Marco, west wall of south transept. The Doge attending the transfer of the body of St Mark. Thirteenth century.
The earliest representation of a cross-section of the basilica.

77 VENICE: S. Marco, north atrium. St Geminianus and St Catherine. Sixteenth century.
Designed by Titian and executed by Zuccato. An example of the dominating role of painters and painterly style during the decline of medieval mosaic art.

78 MINIATURE MOSAIC. The twelve festivals of the Church. Byzantine, early fourteenth century. 16 x 27 cm. (excluding frame). Opera del Duomo, Florence. One of a pair of book covers, framed in gold and silver, containing six panels each. Miniature tesserae of various materials on wax base. For the Nativity scene, cf. *pls 48–50*.

79 ANCIENT MEXICO. Turquoise mosaic incrustation on a human skull, probably representing Tezcatlipoca, the god of the night sky. Mixtec work. Date uncertain. Turquoise; black areas, lignite; eyes, convex discs of iron pyrites set in white shell. 16.5 x 15 cm. British Museum, London.

48

49

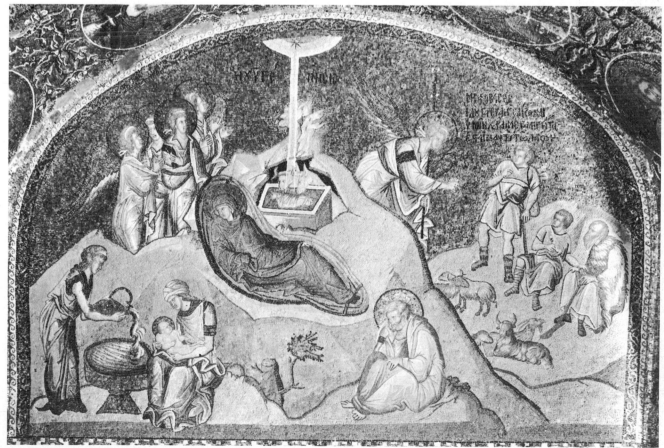

50

51

52

53

54

55

56

57

58

59

60

61

62

63

64

66

67

68

69

70

71

72

73

74

76

77

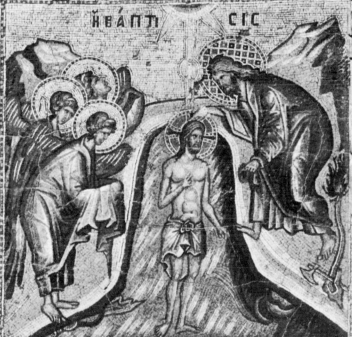

78

Third Phase: Modern Expansion

A revival of mosaic is now in progress. The medium has attained a far wider geographical spread than ever before, and a far greater range of styles, techniques and subject-matter. Like other media today, it has split into two clearly discernible streams, one traditionalist and one experimental, with a whole gamut of varieties in between. It is characteristic of the conservative nature of mosaic that its modern development initially sprang from the desire to restore or to imitate the heritage of the past. This fact has been, and still is, a help to mosaic in practical and technical terms, but an aesthetic hindrance.

The continuance of the technical tradition from which this third phase of mosaic was to evolve was in fact linked with one of the major causes of decline in the preceding phase: the imitation of painting. It occurred to a seventeenth-century pope that the oil and fresco paintings in the Vatican basilica might be replaced by mosaic replicas, which would be more durable. This idea was put into practice when, in 1727, Benedict XIII established a permanent papal workshop which survives to this day in the *Reverenda Fabbrica di S. Pietro*. In time the Vatican's own smalti factory came to produce no less than 28,000 shades – more than enough to render each and every nuance on the painter's palette – and with them mosaicists were able to produce facsimiles of paintings by Guercino, Guido Reni, Raphael and Domenichino amongst others. Raphael's 'Transfiguration', which visitors admire in the basilica, is in fact a mosaic copy of the original painting now kept in the Pinacoteca Vaticana. The copies are very accurate, except that the size of some of the pictures has been adapted by means of an intermediate working cartoon (see pp. 145–6) to make them fit better into the architectural setting, and the unsuspecting eye is easily deceived by the virtually unbroken and quite oily looking surfaces of what are, no doubt, triumphs of skilled precision. The trouble is that they are neither true paintings no true mosaics. In course of time this studio and others went on meticulously to reproduce pictures by Caravaggio, Rembrandt and Gauguin, and various versions and variations of Leonardo's *Last Supper* can be seen in Vienna, London, Liverpool, and presumably also elsewhere. To the credit of the Vatican studio, however, it must be stated that it now looks back with wry amusement on such misguided applications of its art.

By the late eighteenth century, when the Vatican was no longer able to keep its twelve mosaicists busy, they began to take on non-ecclesiastical work. In an age of antiquarian interest, they found plenty of wealthy customers prepared to buy replicas of classical mosaics, and they are said to have exported hundreds of copies of the famous mosaic of the pigeons (*pl. 7*). A new and much larger task suddenly came their way when, in 1823, the fire in S. Paolo fuori le mura destroyed most of the basilica's extensive mosaic decoration dating from the fifth to the thirteenth centuries. Its restoration – or decoration afresh – was followed by repairs in other churches where brittle mosaics had begun to crumble off, among them S. Costanza, S. Maria in Trastevere, the Lateran basilica, the cathedrals at Grottaferrata, Salerno and Orvieto.

The *Sanpietrini* and other Italians during the nineteenth century also passed their skill on to other nations like the Greek masters of earlier ages. In Russia, the poet Lomonosov, assisted by the painter Vassiliev, had made some brave but crude experiments around 1755 with mosaic portraits of Peter the Great and the Tsarina Elizabeth, but more lasting impetus was provided by F. Solntsev's rediscovery around 1843, during restorations to the frescos in Sv. Sophia at Kiev, of Byzantine mosaics which had been hidden under plaster. Not long after this, in 1846, Tsar Nicholas I, with the Holy See's co-operation, established a mosaic workshop in Rome. Russians were trained there by Italians, and when the studio was moved to St Petersburg six years later, several of the tutors accompanied it. Among work produced in the Tsar's capital are the four large figures in St Isaac's Cathedral. Soon, however, the studio was integrated into the Academy of Fine Arts, and mosaic and its teaching virtually became a province of painting. There, apparently, the matter has rested in Russia. In 1945, sixty truck-loads of smalti from the Berlin mosaic factory were carted off by the victorious Russians and were presumably put to some use, though no information on any modern developments is available from Soviet authorities and institutions. Mosaics designed by celebrated painters such as Alexander Deineka (1899–1969) observe the hagiographic attitudes of Socialist Realism, which is quite unsuited to the medium, but official art doctrine seems to have blocked any awareness of the propaganda value to be gained by truly revolutionary and popular mosaic art of the kind developed with so much panache in Mexico.

In France, a Florentine named Migliorini kept a studio during the seventeenth century, but does not seem to have been very active. It was Napoleon, eager to add to the lustre of his new crown, who, in 1804, established an imperial mosaic workshop headed by another Italian, Francesco Belloni, who had formerly been in the papal service. The most important work he and his deaf-and-dumb assistants carried out is a large and technically accomplished pavement in the Melpomene Room of the Louvre. Its classical style and allegorical manner are characterized by the title under which it was exhibited in 1810: *Le Génie de l'Empereur maîtrisant la Victoire et ramenant la Paix et l'Abondance*. In going back to antiquity, mosaic was also, after hundreds of years, returning to non-religious uses, and this process of resecularization was to extend its scope during the nineteenth and twentieth centuries. At first mosaic was still under the monarch's patronage, but redemocratization was soon to follow, eventually, albeit very slowly, affecting both style and technique. Belloni's workshop kept going for about thirty years. Under the Third Republic, the expert and enthusiastic Edouard Gerspach – whose book on mosaics (1881), though out of date, remains unsurpassed – again secured government support for an *Ecole nationale de la mosaïque*. This was set up in 1876, again under the direction of an ex-papal master mosaicist, Poggesi, and among its works was the apse in the Panthéon. However, this school, too, did not exist for more than a few decades, and some of France's largest mosaic decorations – in the Paris Opéra and in Marseilles Cathedral – were not in fact carried out by French workshops, but by a Venetian firm which had emerged as the world's supplier of mosaics.

Mosaic Industrialized

Dr Antonio Salviati (1816–90), a lawyer by training, did more than anyone else to spread the ancient art of mosaic by putting it on an industrial and commercial basis. Around 1860, supported by the technical expertise of Lorenzo Radi (1803–74), a Murano glass-maker who re-examined the composition and colouring of smalti, Salviati injected new vitality into Venice's glass and mosaic trade. As far as can be discovered, he was the first to introduce the 'indirect' system of setting tesserae on a temporary paper base (see p. 146), thus enabling a complete mosaic to be pre-assembled at a central point before being shipped to its final site – and this was the secret of his workshop's success. Because of the surface flatness it produces, the method was not particularly beneficial to the quality of the restoration work on the wall mosaics in St Mark's, for which his company had the concession for a time. One of his richest fields of cultivation, however, was Queen Victoria's golden England, and indeed that proud and pompous pinnacle of the period, the Albert Memorial in Kensington Gardens, was decorated by the Salviati workshop. For its German equivalent, the Siegessäule in Berlin, a series of scenes commemorating the foundation of the Bismarck Reich was faithfully translated into mosaic from cartoons by the painter Anton von Werner. The work of Salviati's men, like that of their Venetian ancestors during the Renaissance, was technically competent, and the principles of the medium were observed as far as could be expected within the limits of the paint-and-brush cartoons supplied to them by their clients: the kings of Rumania, Egypt and Siam, Russian Grand Dukes, Berlin bankers and churches in New York and Palo Alto, California, in Buenos Aires and Sydney.

Mosaic had now been drawn into the industrial age; but it kept aloof from the aesthetic revolution which Cézanne, Monet, Seurat and Gauguin were bringing about at the same time and which was so closely related to its own nature. Such current movements in art as did affect mosaic were, significantly, those which were associated with styles of the past: the influence of the Pre-Raphaelites, for example, can be seen in the decoration of the American church in Via Nazionale in Rome, executed after designs by Sir Edward Burne-Jones; and Art Nouveau, which had obvious affinities with the decorative effects and elongated figures of the Middle Ages, has left its mark on some of the vaults of St Paul's in London. Form and subject matter remained academic and archaizing, since nineteenth-century thinking regarded mosaic as distinctly and definitely a medieval form of art – a view that persists even in the second half of the twentieth century, particularly among ecclesiastical patrons.

This attitude was still the order of the day when Salviati's enterprise was emulated in Germany. Three young Berliners discovered by their own experiments the methods of smalti manufacture which were so jealously guarded by the Venetians. In 1889 they founded a factory which was to operate until 1969 in its palatial neo-Romanesque building directly adjoining what had by then been turned into the Berlin Wall. Wagner's was probably the sole company in modern times not only to produce smalti (in 15,000 shades), but also, under the same roof, to compose mosaics by the indirect system for shipment throughout the world. The huge surfaces of the Kaiser Wilhelm Memorial Church in Berlin were covered with regiments of Hohenzollern ancestors in the neo-romantic and neo-Byzantine taste of the turn of the century. Nevertheless, August Wagner, the head of the firm for many years, was aware that imitation of painting was 'undoubtedly a violation of the style' (as he said in 1898), and sought to establish a close working association with designing artists able to understand the medium. Thus, thanks to Wagner and others, the styles and the subjects of the twentieth century gradually began to be reflected in mosaic.

Modernization of Style

The history of the Wagner workshop provides notable examples of this widening and modernization of style: the Dutch artist Jan Thorn Prikker (1868–1932) translated conventional Christian iconography into the idiom of modern expressionism (*pl. 82*) and the Swede Einar Forseth (b. 1892), in the Golden Room of the Stockholm city hall (1921–3), used mosaic to illuminate Nordic myths with the glow of Byzantium. The Berlin company supplied not only churches and palaces, but banks, offices, hospitals, even ships – an idea first practised in ancient Syracuse. In 1923 a branch company, grandly named 'Ravenna Mosaic Company, Inc.', was set up in the United States (where it now operates independently), and in 1932 Wagner mosaicists depicted a pageant of Indian chiefs and other figures from America's past and present in Cincinnati's Union Terminal station. At about the same time, they began the extensive work (interrupted by the war and resumed around 1960) of covering the interior of the Roman Catholic cathedral in St Louis with traditional images in the Byzantine-Sicilian manner, where, however, haloed saints were happily joined by modern Americans in lounge suits.

XI ANTONI GAUDÍ (1852–1926). Finial on the Cathedral of the Sagrada Familia at Barcelona. *c.* 1925.
One of the last designs of the Catalan architect and prophet of Art Nouveau for the church with which he was concerned from 1883 until his death. In covering his curved buildings with mosaics (in this case, broken tiles), he became a pioneer of twentieth-century mosaic in three senses: the decoration of large exterior surfaces, the application of mosaic to sculptural shapes, and the use of inexpensive materials in irregular fragments.

XII FERNAND LÉGER (1881–1955). Façade of the Musée Fernand Léger at Biot, Alpes-Maritimes. Designed 1954. 90 x 440 cm.
Originally intended for the Niedersachsenstadion at Hanover (see *pl. 86*). Smalti, which form the background surface, are combined in a novel way with the tiles used for the figurative portions, whose contours stand out in relief and cast shadows.

XII

An independent artist who worked out his own approach to new forms and themes was Boris Anrep (1883–1969), a Russian who had settled in Paris after World War I and who worked on numerous London commissions (using the indirect system). He was one of the first mosaicists in modern times to design his own cartoons as well as to execute them with his assistants. Much of his output inevitably consisted of highly competent and convincing imitations of Byzantine murals (for instance, in Westminster Cathedral and in the little Greek cathedral in Bayswater) and he also provided floors for the Bank of England, the National Gallery and the Tate Gallery. Roger Fry perceptively praised his pavement in a house in Upper Brook Street where, for once, he had a chance to treat a contemporary subject: the daily life of a fashion-conscious and telephone-loving lady of 1922 London society. He did so in the flat, vigorous shapes of modern expressionism – though still retaining a link with models from late antiquity, for his stylistic advances were based on a profound study of the traditions of mosaic art.

Among major modern painters associated with mosaic, Gino Severini had a feeling for the medium which was rooted in his divisionist and Futurist background and which he deepened by collaborating with the masters of mosaic technique in modern Ravenna. This insight is noticeable even in his comparatively conventional murals for the church of St Pierre in the Swiss town of Fribourg, with their angular figures and coarse tesserae in bold arrangement. It is even more obvious in a composition strongly influenced by Futurism like the 1952 still-life (*pl. 81*). There is no reason to overrate Severini's contribution to mosaic art; he did not achieve any major advances in the medium, and the school of mosaic which he ran in Paris in his later years does not seem to have left any significant mark. But he was nevertheless aware of the importance to the medium of an 'accord between theme and craft', and he noted in his lecture at Ravenna in 1952 that, 'Today, alas, such accord is usually absent. It cannot exist when the art is expected from one person and the craft from another.'

This is very true, and even a great painter's name on the cartoon is far from guaranteeing a successful mosaic. Braque in his last work, a mosaic design for St Gallen, found the right note of bold simplicity but did not take full advantage of the subtler possibilities of the medium (*pl. 91*). Matisse, whose decorative talent made use of such related techniques as tiled walls and coloured paper collages, never turned his hand to mosaic and may not have felt that small tesserae were suitable for his broad shapes – although this seems a pity, to judge from the translation of a Matisse motif by William Ruder, with its sensitive arrangement of the tesserae (*pl. 92*). Mosaics, both figurative and abstract, which Léger designed during his last years, decorate the churches at Assy and Audincourt, the American war memorial at Bastogne in Belgium, the universities of Mexico and Venezuela and the façade of the Musée Léger at Biot. Léger helped to extend the medium by combining classic smalti with other materials, in his case large ceramic tiles, which are used for the figures that stand out in relief from the background of the mosaic (*pl. XII*). But his large flat areas, covered with tesserae of a single colour rather than being enlivened by mixing different hues, might just as well consist of solid sheets, and this suggests that Léger's understanding of the medium was not much better than that of some of his distinguished fellow painters, past and present. Among these, Chagall can serve as a warning example – or so one must hope – of a celebrated painter who dashes his soft, sketchy lines indiscriminately down on paper when he is supposed to be planning a solid floor composed of hard, angular tesserae. He thus requires the practical mosaicist to perform a task quite uncongenial to the nature of his medium – as becomes embarrassingly clear from a comparison between his cartoon and the finished (pseudo-) mosaic in the Knesset (*pls 89–90*).

By contrast, the versatile Swiss artist Hans Erni, who, like Severini, was helped by the expertise of the Ravenna workshop in producing his ambitious mural for the Berne broadcasting building, has not only linked the worlds of mythology and technology, but also managed to integrate both flat and modelled elements by means of a graphic network of white lines (*pl. XIII*). Hans Stocker, another Swiss, kept to traditional Christian figures (the Virgin at Solothurn, or Christ in Majesty in the new Kaiser Friedrich Memorial Church in Berlin), but the principle of mosaic, the assemblage of polychrome particles, is applied in a novel way by breaking the heavenly figure up into a vision of flurrying sparks (*pl. 83*).

It is a measure of the wide spread and diversity of mosaic-making today that it is impossible to mention more than a few of those who, while still using the ancient technique, are combining it with new styles inspired by movements in contemporary painting – from the realistically figurative, through various degrees of stylization and distortion, to the purely abstract. There are followers of Picasso or Matisse, like the Brazilian painter Emiliano Di Cavalcanti who designed the 150 ft frieze depicting the performing arts on the façade of the Teatro de Cultura Artística in São Paulo. There is the excellent Carlos Mérida from Guatemala who has applied the principles of Orphism to mosaic – long after Delaunay but as logically and classically as few others. Both objects and background are simplified to such an extent that they can almost be read as abstract structures made up of intersecting colour planes, and these works come close to Mérida's purely non-representational mosaics. Helmut Lander, possibly the most perceptive designer of mosaics active in Germany, used an analogous approach in his early mural on Greek themes in the Ludwig Georg School at Darmstadt.

Abstract cartoons tend to be especially congenial to the flat medium of mosaic. Jean Bazaine, the abstract expressionist, has, within the terms of his style, given impressive expression even to religious concepts in the façade of the Audincourt church (1951). Lee Krasner, Jackson Pollock's widow, designed the huge *sopraporta* murals at the Uris Building in New York and, together with her nephew Ronald Stein, personally took part in their execution (1959). These examples suggest that the work of artists such as Mark Rothko or Peter Sedgley, and particularly of Hard Edge painters like Robyn Denny or Frank Stella, might prove eminently suitable for mosaic adaptation if architects had the sense to enlist the artists' interest.

The subtleties of *andamento* and of shades of colour can perhaps be measured and mastered with ideal sensitivity only if it is the designer's own finger which presses the tesserae into the plaster. This was the case, for example, when Augusto Ranocchi was producing his mural in the Rome office of Iberia Airlines. In style the work resembles an action painting – but naturally the method is not quite the same as that of action painting, for the spontaneity which has created the cartoon is not easily maintained through the lengthy process of assembling the tesserae, and, to rekindle it, the designer's personal participation and free interpretation of the cartoon is doubly important.

Exceptionally, the ideal of art-craft unity can gain an additional dimension if the designer-mosaicist is intimately familiar with the production and properties of his material. A rather unexpected case is that of Rokuro Yabashi (b. 1905), who trained as a painter both in his native Japan and in Europe and is now director of the marble company founded by his father at Gifu. The numerous and often very large wall and floor mosaics he and his assistants have created for buildings all over the country are typically Japanese – even in the eclectic use of figurative and abstract styles current in the West. Yabashi has said, 'I was born with stones, brought up among stones, and paint with stones', and his delicate Japanese sense of colour is clearly and closely linked with his experience in the selection and treatment of coloured stones, which he supplements only occasionally by smalti.

Glass tesserae are, of course, the favourite material of the Orsoni brothers, whose working day is spent in blue overalls by the melting furnace in their smalti factory in Venice. In a little studio above their factory, however, they use their tesserae in various aesthetic experiments, and are discovering new extensions of the traditional form (*pl. 94*). Lucio Orsoni's most recent work (which was represented at the 1970 Biennale in Venice) reduces mosaic to the abstract purity of *andamento* lines, heightened only by the subtle contrast between rows of white and of gold smalti and by almost imperceptibly graded shades of both colours: a style born directly of the traditional techniques of smalti production and setting, yet at the same time closely related to contemporary Hard Edge abstraction.

The inherent affinity of the medium with certain modern trends such as Op Art is underlined by the fact that these potentialities have been realized independently by more than one artist in very similar ways. Orsoni arrived at his new style without any knowledge of the work done a few years earlier in New York by Aleksandra Kasuba (*pl. 104*), whose completely monochrome abstract murals of rough-cut black marble tesserae have achieved a harmonious balance of bold experiment and classic technique. Theme, movement, even an appearance of tonal grading within the strictly monochrome surface – everything is accomplished exclusively by means of the *andamento* of the tesserae and their gradually widening interstices. Changing light intensifies and modifies the Op Art effect by which the artist is trying to explore the illusion of space and time. With austere economy, renouncing even colour contrasts, she has distilled the essence of mosaic.

Ravenna Today

But it is Ravenna which has once again become the citadel of the finest technical tradition. In the past the monuments of the city's glory were liable to suffer from repairs, or even 'improvements', inspired by the taste of the day. Modern standards of conservation, however, demanded painstaking respect for the original, based on a careful study of the early Christian technique with its direct system of application and its colour and light effects. It was undoubtedly with the training of competent restorers in mind that, in 1926, the Academy of Fine Arts in Ravenna established a mosaic class where students from all over the world are today receiving free instruction from Professors Renato and Carlo

Signorini (father and son). Pupils even younger are being trained at Ravenna's admirable *Istituto Statale d'Arte per il Mosaico* (established in 1959), a secondary school with a special bias towards mosaic classes, and its counterpart at Monreale. Another important mosaic college has been operating since 1921 at Spilimbergo in Friuli, and in Venice the INIASA school was set up in 1968 with Antonio Orsoni among its teachers.

The main occupation in the Ravenna studios is no longer restoration work but the making of copies – copies of the large Theodora group from S. Vitale for the world's museums and of small heads of saints to be taken home by tourists – and these replicas are both a blessing and a curse. A curse because they hamper original work and a blessing, not only because they are a steady source of income, but also because they compel the copying artists to study every single tessera of the masterpieces they are re-producing. This form of direct tuition from the ancient masters has turned the copyists themselves into superb masters of mosaic technique. Their original work, too, with the glittering yet velvet-soft sheen of their tesserae setting, can hold its own with the finest of ancient Ravenna – take Hans Erni's mural in Berne (*pl. XIII*), or the panorama of the history of Tel Aviv designed by Nachum Gutman (*pl. XIV*). In parts of the latter the artists of the *Gruppo Mosaicisti*, working in close association with the Israeli painter, have introduced into the large mural some discreet departures from the traditional technique; certain portions are picked out in relief, and some of the grout filling the joints is coloured to contrast with the tesserae and emphasize the effect of the joints and the separateness of the tesserae. Resourcefully, these Ravenna virtuosi have also demonstrated their ability to enter into the spirit of a very different type of art when, in collaboration with the *tachiste* painter Georges Mathieu, they rendered his strands and blotches of paint by continuous strips and lumps of glass, applied in liquid state and then allowed to set – thus obtaining genuine spontaneity rather than a skilful imitation of it. Yet, even in cases like these, the Ravenna artists are merely using their talents to carry out someone else's designs.

XIII   Hans Erni (b. 1909). *Ut omnia exsolvantur*. Mural in the Radio and Television Building in Berne (detail). 1964. Smalti.
In a complex cosmological composition, the Swiss painter combines classical mythology with phenomena of modern technology, such as communications satellites (as he has also done in the decorative pattern of punched computer cards in a very similar mural for an insurance building at Winterthur in 1970). The white lines of the figures and the quasi-abstract colour areas form largely independent yet interacting planes, and the formal boldness of combining them owes much of its success to the imaginative and varied execution of details by the *Gruppo Mosaistici* workshop in Ravenna.

XIV   Nachum Gutman (b. 1898 in Russia, in Palestine since 1905). Detail from the mural in the Shalom Mayer Tower in Tel Aviv representing the history of the city. 1965–6. Smalti (8000 shades), total area of mural about 4.8 x 17 m.
During the execution, in the workshop of the *Gruppo Mosaistici* in Ravenna with the Israeli painter's assistance, certain portions of the surface were raised in relief. The huge mural was composed by the direct system in a number of rectangular sections which were later joined up on the site.

XIII

XIV

The courage to break new ground tends to occur more frequently in artists not committed to any tradition by a specific training in mosaic. Their adventurous imagination can extend the medium, though, on the other hand, it may result in self-indulgent charlatanism and indiscipline. The best of both worlds could be combined if expert mosaicists, like those in Ravenna, borrowed some of that drive and enterprise, for they, who can sense the movement of the tesserae in their finger-tips, are better equipped than others to be designers as well as technicians, to create work of their own and to develop new styles. But they are so pre-occupied with their devoted service to Ravenna's great past and with their technical perfection that, even in the case of commissions for contemporary decoration, they usually rely on designs supplied by other hands – by painters. This is the curse of intimate intercourse with an overwhelming tradition.

Apart from this psychological problem, there is also a practical one. The magnificence and munificence of kings and churches having dwindled, there are few patrons today who can afford expensive smalti and the labour-intensive application of tiny tesserae in large-scale decoration work. Thus, mosaic of the classic type does not get many opportunities to play its full architectural role; by and large, its symphonic breadth has shrunk to the chamber-music of limited ornamental panels.

Nevertheless, the classic technique is not dead, for the examples mentioned so far, including those in modern and even experimental styles, are almost wholly based on traditional smalti traditionally put together. But this is no longer the only technique. Major advances have been brought about outside the centres of tradition and by outsiders who, while receiving inspiration from tradition, have developed it with new materials and methods – a process not unlike the transition from antiquity to the Middle Ages.

Impetus from Art Nouveau

One impulse came from the direction of Art Nouveau. Gustav Klimt's paintings from the period of the Vienna *Secession* show on the one hand quasi-pointillistic areas built up from multi-coloured flowers and leaves, and on the other a taste for Byzantine decorativeness, for gold grounds and for the insertion of coloured stones analogous to those used by the masters of S. Vitale (see the mother-of-pearl pieces in the figure of Theodora, *pl. 42*). It was not long after Klimt's visit to Ravenna of 1903 that all these features appeared together in his mural decoration for the dining-room in the Brussels house of the coal tycoon Stoclet (designed 1905–9; *pl. 80*): a montage of smalti mosaic, painted portions and patterned tiles, as well as preformed ceramic shapes recalling *opus sectile*. The definition of mosaic can hardly be stretched far enough to accommodate so heterogeneous a mixture as this. Nonetheless, it was the principle of such a mixture that was later to introduce greater flexibility into true mosaics. Klimt himself never took more than the initial step.

Antoni Gaudí went further (*pl. XI*). The Catalan architect and prophet of Art Nouveau was not merely concerned with the shapes of his buildings in and around Barcelona but equally with their outside surfaces, which he wanted to contribute an effect of their own. There was no better means of accentuating architectural features than colour, and the Hispano-Moresque tradition of glazed tiles was an obvious choice. He used both the monochrome and the individually patterned type, frequently in broken pieces. For variety he added fragments of glass bottles and china plates, even such *objets trouvés* as a doll's head, and alternated such relatively large units with small smalto tesserae. While the elegant Klimt had many components specially made for his Stoclet montage, Gaudí made use of debris and waste matter, just as Kurt Schwitters was to do in his *Merz* pictures. He thus demonstrated that it was possible to decorate large surfaces with very cheap materials which, because the pieces tend to be rather larger than tesserae, has the added advantage of saving time and money in fixing. These fragments could be made to fit like a skin round all the curious curves of his buildings and, since his adventurous architecture was essentially a form of sculpture, he was also leading the way towards mosaic-coated sculpture – an application of the medium which had hardly ever been thought of in Europe before. Whereas during the Middle Ages mosaic had been concerned almost solely with church interiors, Gaudí gave it an exterior role – a technical departure which is symbolic of the changeover from an introverted and religious attitude to a more extrovert and secular one. Gaudí's personal work may have been that of a lone eccentric, but it was to prove seminal – particularly for the striking development of mosaic in Latin America.

Tradition and Revolution in Mexico

It could be that Gaudí himself had drawn some inspiration from the long history of mosaic in pre-Columbian America. There seem to have been two separate traditions: one in Peru and one in Mexico. In Peru small implements were given mosaic incrustations of bone, ivory, shell, copper carbonate and gold. In Mexico the Olmec ruins at La Venta, dating from as early as the first millennium BC, include two mosaic-type floors of serpentine slabs and coloured clays representing the characteristic jaguar mask, and a literary source mentions mosaic murals at Tula. Surviving walls in the Zapotec city of Mitla (*c.* AD 800), however, cannot really be called mosaic, consisting as they do of monochrome rectangular stones, some protruding and some receding, arranged to form geometric weaving patterns. The Mayas and the Aztecs certainly coated ritual objects (sacrificial knives, shields, helmets, figures, wooden masks and, occasionally, human skulls representing deities) with tesserae made of various semi-precious stones, often very small and thin (*pl. 79*). In some cases, graded shades of colour do occur; but there is no juxtaposing of contrasting colours, and the tesserae do not form patterns or images, so that the resulting effect is not that of mosaic in the European sense. An odd fact is that the prevalence of turquoise is reminiscent of the popularity of blue mosaic in Spain, the country of the future conquerors – a parallel which has no doubt facilitated the harmonious fusion of native tradition with European models in modern Mexican mosaic.

Latin America's climate and landscape encourage colourful exterior decoration, and the low cost of manpower for the time-consuming work of setting permits a bit more to be spent on materials. Authorities have promoted public building and the arts, realizing that the arts, employed in a popular manner, can promote national identity and that they are useful as propaganda tools, just as mosaic was in the medieval Church. Boundaries between the various arts are still open, and artists are flexible, moving easily between one medium and another. Moreover, the powerful and colourful idiom of Mexico's 'social realist' painters has an affinity with the idiom of mosaic, and, as a result, modern Mexican painting and mosaic were born as twins.

Diego Rivera, in the façade he designed in 1951 for the Teatro de los insurgentes, depicted the country's history in popular scenes which anticipate some of the naïve brightness of Pop Art (*pl. XV*). The medium is handled sensitively, though conventionally, but what is lacking is any real attempt at integrating the huge frieze with the architecture. However, Rivera achieved a triumph of true genius in his mosaic environment outside the Mexico City waterworks, where the mighty figure of the rain god Tlaloc and its surrounding area are covered with natural stones of various shapes and colours (*pls 96–7*). This masterly continuation and consummation of the principles underlying Gaudí's whimsical fantasy is perhaps the greatest modern work of mosaic.

Mexico can also claim to possess the biggest modern mosaic decoration (*pl. 98*). The murals covering all four sides of the library tower of the University of Mexico were designed by a friend of Rivera's, Juan O'Gorman, who, as an architect by profession, has also been responsible (with two colleagues) for the design of this big box of a building. It would seem an ideal conjunction of functions but, unhappily, O'Gorman the architect has completely abdicated his task of shaping the building to O'Gorman the muralist – who has failed to fulfil it. His mosaics as such (particularly those elsewhere) are imaginative and successful but, in the case of the library, the pictorial wrapping-paper, which disrupts rather than supports the lines and surfaces of the building, is a monument of anti-architectural mosaic decoration. Its lesson seems to be that the two roles of architect and muralist are better left to separate personalities working in dialectical interaction.

The early 1950s turned Mexico City into a veritable showcase of contemporary mosaic, containing also mosaic reliefs by Rivera (*pl. 103*) and Siqueiros (*pl. 102*), expressive scenes by José Chávez Morado and elegant abstractions by Armando Barrios, André Bloc, Pascual Navarro and Oswaldo Vigas, as well as by Fernand Léger. This great volume of work in Mexico, and other Latin American countries, would hardly have been possible had there not been an alternative to expensive smalti in the cheaper materials and the mixed techniques which Gaudí had pioneered. These new methods are becoming increasingly popular all over the world and, while the need for economy from which they arise has vulgarized mosaic in some cases, it has also revitalized its form and its style.

New Methods and Materials

Even smalti can be applied in a way which saves time and money and offers an additional stylistic device if, instead of (or in combination with) small tesserae, larger pieces in random shapes are used. Seen from a distance, these are even likely to enhance rather than to diminish the effect of a mural. Naturally this method involves using the larger top surface of the smalto 'pancake' (see p. 143), which is smooth, and thus loses the more interesting reflecting properties of the narrow and uneven cut face; but there is some compensation in the fact that darker-coloured marbling and glass bubbles in the surface can make a vivid effect which is largely excluded in a small tessera.

Another possibility is setting figures composed of polychrome tesserae into an otherwise plain plastered wall to obtain a more informal effect, akin to that of a drawing or print. In practice this method is chosen mainly for its simplicity and the saving in material and labour. But some artists are using plain areas of coloured plaster for contrast within a smalti composition, among them Johannes Schreiter (*pl. 87*) and Carlo Signorini.

A related principle also forms the basis of the highly experimental work of the New York artist Jeanne Reynal (b. 1903). As an assistant to Boris Anrep, she had gained a thorough grounding in the traditional technique before embarking, around 1950, on a true equivalent of action painting in terms of mosaic. Not unlike Jackson Pollock dribbling and splashing paint on canvas, she scatters glass or marble tesserae loosely over a soft plaster bed and then adjusts some of the angles at which they have fallen, creating instant mosaics with mottled surfaces roughly comparable to Dubuffet's *Texturologies*. The sweep of her hand is analogous to the flowing movement of a brush, and at the same time introduces an element of chance – two factors which are quite alien to the usual laborious procedures of mosaic art. What remains to be seen is whether Jeanne Reynal's bold experiment will lead to more than textural effects.

Among the new and cheaper materials which are widely available commercially, vitreous mosaic is perhaps the most important (see p. 144–5). These mass-produced and standardized tesserae do not differ very much from the costlier smalti either in chemical composition or in application except that, being thinner, they are less suited for varying angles and glittering reflections. They are supplied on paper backing-sheets, either monochrome or in colourful random mixtures, ready for immediate fitting as an unassuming but attractive facing for interior or exterior walls. Alternatively, stylized, angular figures can be built up on a grid system out of these precise little coloured squares. This pictorial use of strict *opus tessellatum* or *reticulatum* is perfectly in keeping with the nature of the material, and it is surprising that so very little use has been made of this logical application of what is, after all, the basic idea of mosaic: a picture composed of equiform units.

XV DIEGO RIVERA (1886–1957). Detail from the scenes of Mexican history and theatre on the façade of the Teatro de los insurgentes, Mexico City. 1951–3.
The scenes and figures are essentially flat in form and arrangement, and their effect results from the bright colours, the stylization and the popular manner. The seams between the sections in which the mosaic was set remain visible. The mural covers a large, gently curved, unarticulated surface, but is not integrated with the architecture.

XVI HANS UNGER and EBERHARD SCHULZE (b. 1915 and 1938 in Germany, living in London). Mosaic in the London boardroom of the ERF commercial vehicles company. 1966. Smalti, fragments of tiles with coloured enamel fused on to the surface, vehicle parts inserted as *objets trouvés*, 105 x 240 cm. (The reproduction is slightly trimmed at the sides.)

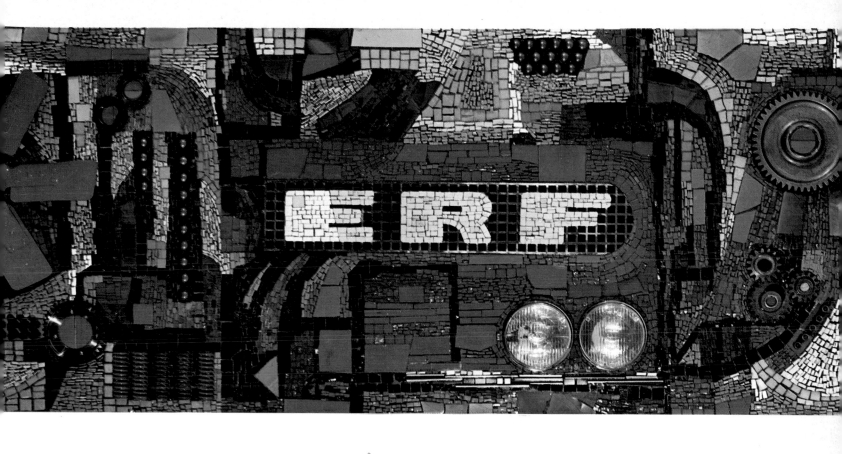

XVI

The same effect can, of course, be obtained with ceramic tesserae (*pl. 95*), the other mosaic material which is supplied by modern industry in large quantities and in a number of formats and colours – either as matt or as glazed tiles. Here again, the variety of shapes and sizes offers the artist a flexible means of expression. There is no other material inexpensive enough to be used for brightening up large outside walls of ordinary residential tower blocks (*pl. 99*). For bathroom walls, prefabricated tile decorations can be ordered by reference number from a catalogue (*pl. 93*) – and why not, after all? Designs created in a big company's art department are likely to be more elegant, and more competent as mosaics, than a small-time tile-fixer's efforts; and it is also worth remembering that industrialization seems to have been hardly less elaborate in Graeco-Roman workshops, with their pattern books and templates for setting tesserae.

A recent idea is that of 'transparent mosaic', in which bits of ordinary coloured glass – either broken pieces or specially manufactured tesserae – are mounted on a glass or Perspex sheet so that a light source behind will activate the colours. Such doors or windows of coloured glass are not the same as stained-glass windows. The fact that, in work of this type, each feature of the design consists of a number of small units places it both technically and formally in the category of mosaic.

Humble bricks, too, are occasionally used quite effectively as larger-scale mosaic components in abstract or even figurative compositions. Much more frequent use is being made of natural stone which, having been cut into cubes for two thousand years, has now acquired new dimensions in more senses than one. Different types of stone are used in pieces of varying size and shape, with the result that their contrasting hues and structures, their rough or polished surfaces, are more fully seen and enjoyed. The abstract murals of Helmut Lander, the versatile German designer, are among the best examples of the dramatic interest and variety that can be added to the austere lines of contemporary architecture by sensitively choosing and juxtaposing the tones and textures of all kinds of stone (*pl. 100*).

While all these materials and methods are fairly common today, there are some isolated artists exploring ways and means of their own. Elena Zarb in London begins at her own kiln by painstakingly firing brilliant earthenware squares and bars, or even preshaped stars or crescents, which she then fits into her stylized panels of saints. At the Oshogbo workshop in Nigeria, Jimoh Buraimoh (b. 1943) has adopted such traditional materials as minute coloured beads from the local market, and sometimes cowries, for mosaic murals and panel pictures, often combining them with areas of flat paint. He is discovering the various patterns and effects of *andamento* to be obtained from the directional arrangement of thin rows of beads, and there is a natural affinity with Byzantine stylization in his expressionistic figures with their broad African presence.

Among *avant garde* experimentalists, there is Glen Michaels in Michigan who makes up abstract expressionist reliefs from wooden printer's reglets or from slate or pebbles – thus linking modern experimentation with mosaic's earliest beginnings.

New idioms are emerging as a result of aesthetic developments, and new materials as a result of industrial and economic developments – and the upshot is that the art of mosaic, once rigidly defined, now enjoys a freedom never known before. While standardized mosaic facings are rolling off conveyor belts, the individual imagination of the artist is challenged to choose between innumerable possibilities. He may well choose a combination, a mixed technique.

Very often this still includes classic smalti for brilliant highlights or fine detail. In the church of the Holy Family in Vienna, Carl Unger has incorporated smalti, tiles and natural stone in various shapes and sizes into a soaring abstract vision of the Heavenly Jerusalem (*pl. 88*). In Johannes Schreiter's pulpit panel at Böblingen near Stuttgart, areas of black plaster are assigned an independent compositional role, at the same time enhancing the brilliance of the red smalti which signify the blood of Christ (*pl. 87*).

These are examples which show church decoration taking resolute strides to catch up with contemporary styles and techniques. They are not without their detractors; some church authorities and church-goers feel that religious themes should be more plainly identifiable. But an evocative abstraction may well spring from a more profoundly spiritual endeavour than worthy routine imitations of traditional iconography or attempts to prolong the life of old images by deforming or transforming them in vaguely modernistic ways. Half-hearted stylistic solutions rarely do justice either to the past or to the present, even if the artist chooses and combines materials as imaginatively as, for example, Karl Knappe (*pl. 85*) who, despite his technical inventiveness, was not really the pioneer of modern church mosaic he has been made out to be. The current uneasiness of church mosaic, as of other religious art, only reflects uncertainties of Christian thought which, while trying to reappraise traditional imagery, has not yet established new and recognizable symbols. Mosaic artists helped to do this in early Christian times, and they may be able to help again if the Church gives them a chance to explore both the medium and the missionary message.

Among the most subtle explorers of the potentialities of mosaic are Hans Unger and his associate Eberhard Schulze in London. By allowing the tesserae to protrude or recede, they have extended the principle of setting them at varying angles, thus adding to the play of light the effect of the shadows cast by these three-dimensional elements. They have combined smalti with marble, stone, slate or fragments of tile, and have incorporated *objets trouvés* such as the type and printing blocks embodied in the mural at the headquarters of Penguin Books (1964) or the engine parts and headlights in the mural for a commercial vehicles company (*pl. XVI*). Since 1969 they have been pursuing a new style of monochrome mosaic which is related to, though different from, the work of Aleksandra Kasuba and Lucio Orsoni (p. 111). Unger and Schulze introduce three-dimensional features of one kind or another so that the cool elegance of the surface – in marble, smalti, or gleaming aluminium or copper cubes – is enlivened either by making some portions stand out in relief, or by arranging parts of the mosaic on gently rising and sloping planes. (As a *jeu d'esprit*, this abstract scheme was applied quasi-representationally in a white relief mosaic of a street-map which was reproduced as a London Transport poster in 1970.) The basic importance of this kind of work lies not only in adapting patterns of current abstract painting, but more particularly in creating genuine equivalents for them in terms of mosaic, which can then be applied in architecture.

There are still too few architects and patrons who have the inspiration and courage to collaborate closely with inventive mosaic artists. London's imaginative architect's department has commissioned the resourceful Antony Hollaway to design and produce elegantly abstract and gaily figurative decorations for housing estates and playgrounds. If the council's funds do not permit large-scale decoration and require economy in the choice of materials, Hollaway manages to turn necessity into a virtue. Using not only smalti, broken tiles and fragments of coloured glass, but also areas of painted fibreglass and even concrete, he can cleverly combine mosaic with architectural sculpture to create an adventure wall for children to climb about on (*pl. 101*). Under the more opulent conditions of California the expert and versatile mosaicist Joseph Young, in consultation with the architectural offices of Richard J. Neutra and Robert Alexander, was able to produce a complex 80 x 20 ft façade for the Los Angeles County Hall of Records (1952–62). Set in relief against the rough-cut granite wall are slabs of polished granite forming a boldly stylized map of waterways in the district, with the Pacific Ocean represented by green and blue glass tesserae; fresh water runs from bronze cups down the wall, through canal-like grooves, into a narrow moat in which lights are installed to illuminate the mural from below.

Such new departures seem a far cry from classical pavements and medieval vaults, yet they are logical extensions of the mosaic principle of joining similar pieces, and of the collage principle of joining dissimilar pieces. Mixed techniques of this kind are probably the most interesting, and possibly the most promising, development in contemporary mosaic. They can be adapted to meet any architectural requirement, if only architects care to call for it, and are opening up many avenues which will lead mosaic into a rich future – a future which has already begun, if only we will look around to see it.

80 GUSTAV KLIMT (1862–1918). Mural in the dining-room of the Palais Stoclet, Brussels (detail). Designed 1905–09, executed 1911. Mixed technique: smalti, pre-shaped ceramic tiles, painting.

81 GINO SEVERINI (1883–1966). *Still-life* (detail). *c.* 1952. Smalti. Hotel at Cortina d'Ampezzo.
Executed by Ravenna mosaicists.

82 JAN THORN PRIKKER (1868–1932). St Peter (detail from *The Last Supper*). 1927. Smalti. Designed for the church at Duinvoord, Holland, and now in the Oude Kerk, The Hague.
Executed by the August Wagner workshop, Berlin.

83 HANS STOCKER (b. 1896). *Christ in Majesty* (detail). 1957. Smalti. Kaiser-Friedrich-Gedächtniskirche, Berlin.
Executed by the August Wagner workshop, Berlin.

84 ARNO BROMBERGER (b. 1921). *Christ in Majesty* (detail). 1965. Stone, 1100 x 300 cm. Altar mural in the Evangelical church at Hohenlockstedt, Holstein.

85 KARL KNAPPE (1884–1970). *The Risen Christ*. 1954. Stone. Catholic church of St Michael, Frankfurt. Executed by the Franz Mayer'sche Hofkunstanstalt, Munich.

86 EDUARD BARGHEER (b. 1901). Façade of the Niedersachsenstadion, Hanover. 1962–3. Smalti. Height of detail about 1.50 m.
Executed by the August Wagner workshop, Berlin.

87 JOHANNES SCHREITER (b. 1930). Pulpit panel in the Martin-Luther-Kirche at Böblingen, Württemberg. 1960. Smalti (large, irregular fragments from the surface of the 'pancake') and black-tinted plaster, 132 x 73 cm.
Executed by the workshop of Dr. H. Oidtmann, Linnich, Rhineland.

88 CARL UNGER (b. 1915). *The Heavenly Jerusalem*, altar mural in the Kirche zur Heiligen Familie, Vienna (central section). 1965–6. Smalti and other materials. Dimensions of mural 8 x 15 m.
The predominant colours are orange, ultramarine and pale blue.

89–90 MARC CHAGALL (b. 1887). Detail from the cartoon for the pavement in the Knesset building, Jerusalem, and the completed mosaic. 1966.
Executed *in situ* by Italian mosaicists.

91 GEORGES BRAQUE (1882–1963). *Bird*. 1963. Smalti, 150 x 150 cm.
Panel in a corridor of the College of Economics, St Gallen. The cartoon for this mosaic was Braque's last work. The ground is golden yellow; the cross, red; the oval, blue-black; and the bird, white and grey.

92 WILLIAM RUDER (b. 1921) after a motif by HENRI MATISSE (1869–1954). *Bird*. 1967. Smalti, ungrouted, 28 x 39 cm. Private collection, New York.

93 *Sea-horse*. Standard design No 20 132 of the Villeroy & Boch ceramic works, Mettlach, Saar. Glazed ceramic tiles, 61 x 92 cm.

94 LUCIO ORSONI (b. 1939). *Discorso sconclusionato* (Inconclusive Argument). 1966. Smalti with metal extensions, 57 x 45 cm. (excluding metal). Collection of the artist, Venice.

95 DEREK HODGKINSON and COLIN BOWLES. *Thames riverscape with Battersea power station*. 1957. Ceramic tiles, three-quarters of an inch square, in eleven colours, 245 x 38 cm. Collection Carter Tiles Ltd, London.

96–7 DIEGO RIVERA (1886–1957). The rain god Tlaloc. 1952. Stone. Mosaic 'environment' and mosaic sculpture outside the Mexico City waterworks.
(Cf. also *pl. XI*.)

98 JUAN O'GORMAN (b. 1905). Scenes and symbols of Mexican history and civilization on the exterior of the library of the University of Mexico, Mexico City. *c.* 1952. Stone. Length 57.9 m., width 13.7 m., height 35.3 m.

99 KENNETH BARDEN. Exterior mural on a residential tower block in Gosport, Hampshire. 1963. Ceramic tiles, three-quarters of an inch square, produced by Carter Tiles Ltd, Poole, Dorset.

100 HELMUT LANDER (b. 1924). Exterior mural on the Institute of Geology building at Cologne University. 1963. Smalti and various types of stone, 96 sq. m.
Executed by the workshop of W. Derix, Düsseldorf-Kaiserswerth.

101 ANTONY HOLLAWAY (b. 1928). Adventure wall in a playground in London. 1966. Cast concrete and vitreous mosaic, lenght 11 m., height 3 m., thickness 1.35 m.

102 DAVID ALFARO SIQUEIROS (b. 1898). *The people to the university – the university to the people*. *c.* 1953. Vitreous tesserae. Relief mosaic on the administration building of the University of Mexico, Mexico City.

103 DIEGO RIVERA (1886–1957). *The merging of the Spanish and Indian races to form the Mexican nation*. 1952. Stone. Relief mosaic on the lava walls of the Mexico City stadium.

104 ALEKSANDRA KASUBA. *Monochrome mosaic*. 1965. Black Belgian marble on a plywood base, ungrouted, 63.5 cm. square. Private collection, New York.

80

81

82

83

84
85

86

87

88

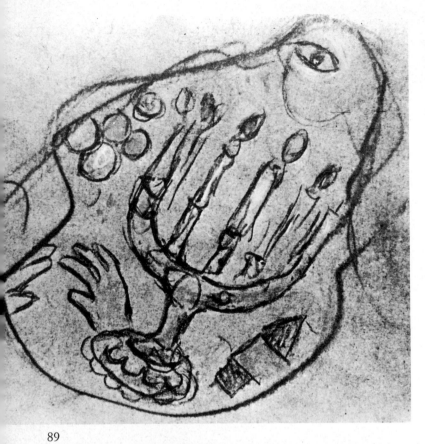

89

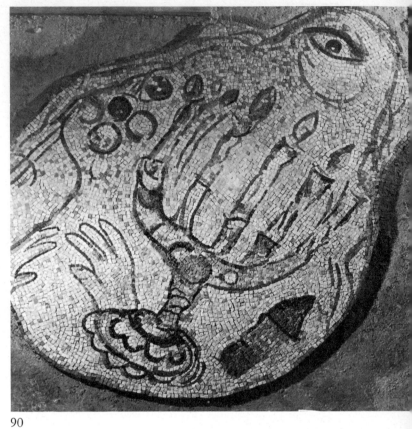

90

91

92

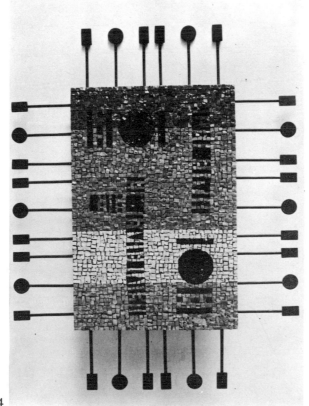

94

95

96

97

99

100

101

102

103

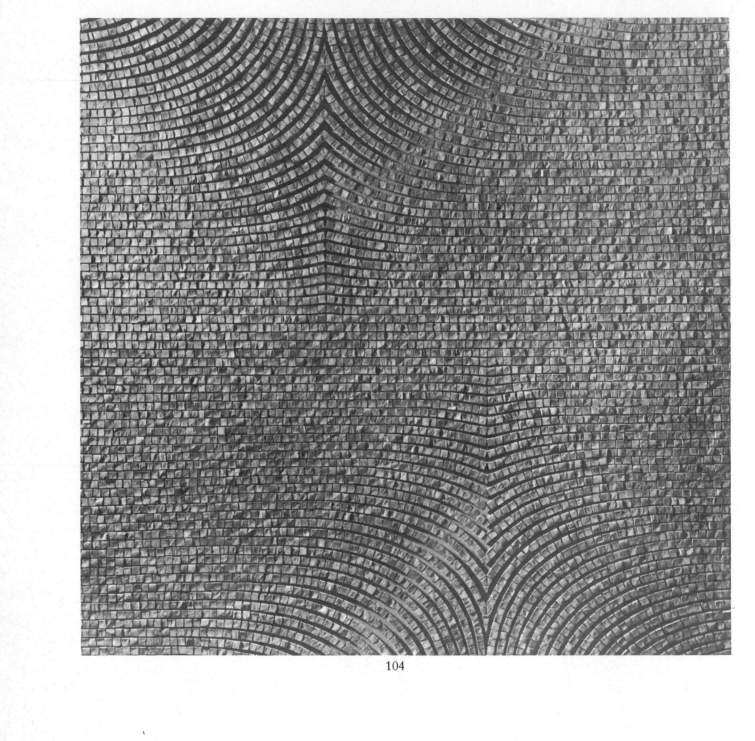

104

Technical Survey: Tesserae and Composition

As technological facts and circumstances have had an essential part to play in shaping the aesthetic character and development of mosaic, an account of its history would not be complete and comprehensible without a systematic survey of its production procedures, particularly as these are generally less well known – to many artists and art experts as well as to laymen – than the techniques of most other artistic media.

Base

The base for a mosaic, unlike a painter's canvas, is not a fixed and finished article. It is produced in the course of the work itself and the mosaicist is able to influence it – as well as to let it influence the artistic form, for example by colouring the 'grout' which joins the tesserae. This is why the preparation of the base is part of the technique of mosaic.

It is a corollary of the architectural origin and purpose of mosaic that this accumulation of hard particles is intended not only to embellish but to strengthen a wall or floor, and classical mosaic, luckily, rested on the firm ground of paving technique. The major Roman sources – Vitruvius and, partly based on him, Pliny – treat mosaic as just a branch of the building trade. In fact, Vitruvius deals with nothing but the foundation, and deals with it very thoroughly, for it is the foundation which has to ensure that the finished surface can withstand weight, wetness and winter frost without warping or subsiding.

Fig. 14 Cross-section of classical pavement foundation: 1 natural soil; 2 *statumen* (rubble bedding); 3 *rudus* (layer of coarse mortar); 4 *nucleus* (fine key layer in which tesserae are embedded); 5 inset tray containing *emblema*; 6 surface of *emblema*; 7 mosaic surface

The ground, after it has been levelled and consolidated, is covered with a thick rubble bedding (*statumen*) of stones 'not smaller than can fill the hand'. Over this is poured a layer of coarse mortar (*rudus*) made of gravel and lime in the proportion of 3:1, or (for open-air pavements) gravel, lime and crushed bricks in the proportion of 2:2:1. This stratum, pounded down thoroughly, must be nine inches thick, or at least a foot if in the open air.

Next comes the key layer (*nucleus*) of fine mortar, consisting of crushed bricks and lime in the proportion of 3:1, at least six inches thick; this provides the bed into which the tesserae are pressed (though some Roman tesserae are not strictly cubes but square pegs, and may go down half an inch or so into the *nucleus*). The interstices between the tesserae are filled in with more mortar, or grout, and the surface is finally levelled and polished with sand. There are, of course, several variants of this procedure.

For mural mosaics the principle of stratified foundation was, and is, applied similarly, but the object is a different one: not to prevent the surface from subsiding, but to prevent individual tesserae from coming loose, or whole patches of the mosaic from becoming detached and forming cavities between the mortar layer and the wall. (The Republic of Venice, in 1648, banned cannon and fireworks within earshot of St Mark's lest the vibration cause damage to the mosaics.) In S. Maria Maggiore, the walls proved too slippery, and the layers of mortar too thick and heavy, while the nails which were intended to support them grew rusty and hastened the deterioration. A good key for the mortar may be provided by roughening the wall with blows of the hammer.

The mortar or cement may consist of powdered marble, slaked lime and *pozzuolana* (a volcanic ash), but there are some other formulae: one, mentioned by Vasari, specifies powdered travertine, crushed bricks and albumen (the latter combining with the lime to impart great strength to the mixture). For better cohesion, straw or other vegetable matter was sometimes added, but this tends to disintegrate with time. The first stratum, which is usually the coarsest, is followed by finer ones (*fig. 15*) – up to four layers have been found in S. Vitale. Each one is allowed to harden, but is then moistened again in order to obtain a bond with the next. The top layer is always applied in patches of a size which the mosaicist is able to cover with tesserae before it sets. The seams between one day's work and the next are discernible in some completed mosaics. In order to delay the drying and setting process and to prolong the time in which adjustments were possible, Muziano da Brescia, working in the Cappella Gregoriana at St Peter's in the late sixteenth century, used a mastic containing oil: 60% powdered travertine, 25% slaked lime (prepared from travertine), 10% raw and 5% boiled linseed oil. A similar formula had apparently been known in Roman times, but its drawback was that stone tesserae tended to absorb the oil and to become discoloured, and that in exterior walls this oil-based mastic was liable to crumble.

It depends on the function and the style of the mosaic how deeply the tesserae are pressed into the plaster, and up to what level, if it all, the interstices are filled with

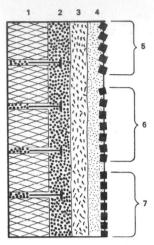

Fig. 15 Cross-section of the structure of a medieval mural mosaic:

1 brick wall; 2 coarse mortar layer with supporting nails; 3 finer mortar layer; 4 finest mortar layer in which tesserae are embedded; 5 tesserae with even surfaces set at parallel angles (used particularly for gold smalti on the higher parts of a wall); 6 tesserae set at different angles (classic technique of mural mosaic); 7 tesserae set parallel and flush with wall (result of indirect setting)

grout. The dark lines made by deep crevices have the aesthetic effect of emphasizing the insular nature of the individual tesserae; on the other hand, in floors and in murals exposed to weather and grime, an unbroken surface, with all joints filled in, is obviously desirable.

Nowadays even large mosaic murals are often completed in the studio, in sections mounted on base panels which are then fixed to the wall by hooks, screws or bolts. The holes left for screws and the gaps or seams where the sections are joined are filled at the site with tesserae reserved for this purpose, and the result is a seamless surface – although this is not invariably done (see *pl. XV*). The same procedure is, of course, indispensable for installing sections produced by the indirect system of tesserae setting (see p. 146).

Ready-made panels are an obvious base for smaller mosaics. Apart from precast concrete panels, various light-weight bases are suitable: plywood (waterproofed to withstand the moisture of the plaster which holds the tesserae), hardboard, asbestos, polyester resin or even stainless metal; in order to provide a grip for the plaster on very smooth surfaces, wire-mesh can be nailed to the base, and this will also have a reinforcing effect. It is also possible simply to glue tesserae to the panel, a method which facilitates adjustments, and in this case grout is applied only at the end to fill in the joints, or the artist may prefer to leave them open. Unfortunately, modern

adhesives, although they have been in use only for a short time, have shown a tendency to warp or crumble off, particularly if applied over a large area. Good old cement mortar still seems to be much the best.

Natural Materials

Virtually any kind of material is suitable for mosaic work. The Sumerians used such natural substances as limestone, lapis lazuli, shell and mother-of-pearl as well as clay; the Aztecs, turquoise and other semi-precious stones; the Greeks, coarse pebbles. At a later stage the Greeks began to chip or cut marble and other types of rock, which offer a surprising variety of colours, into small cubes, thus creating the classic unit of mosaic, the tessera. Its size in antiquity ranged from that of a finger-nail, for coarser work, down to that of a pin-head for minute detail (about two square centimetres down to one square millimetre).

Stone has always remained one of the most important materials, particularly for hard-wearing floors, but it has also been used, alongside smalti, in medieval murals for such purposes as flesh tints. Slate, in various shades, is popular today because of its matt glimmer, especially in larger pieces. Perishable materials, too, can be used to make mosaics: colourful birds' feathers such as the Aztecs used, pieces of wood or bone, shells, and even fruit seeds which children lay out in patterns on the beach or on their desks in school, experiencing in their play the principle of mosaic and the infinite range of its possibilities.

Smalti (Glass Mosaic)

The mosaic material *par excellence*, apart from stone and marble, is the *smalto* tessera, which offers incomparable brilliance and an unlimited choice of colours, besides being weather-resistant. Smalti are basically glass with metal oxides added as colouring agents, and the derivation of the Italian term *smalto*, from the same root as that of 'smelt', indicates that they are the outcome of a melting process. They are alternatively referred to as enamels (a misleading term, as it normally describes only a thin surface coating), glass pastes or glass mosaic – or sometimes as 'artistic', 'Byzantine' or 'Venetian' glass mosaic, although, ironically, this effort to distinguish them from the mass-produced vitreous mosaic (see pp. 144–5) only serves to confuse the two.

The manifold subtleties of shade, texture and consistency in smalti result from subtleties in production which some manufacturers tend to shroud in secrecy – apparently not only to protect them from competitors but also to heighten the lustre of their aristocratic product by adding a touch of mystery. But there is little doubt that there is, in the experienced master-smelter's intuitive 'know-how', an element of white (or rather polychrome) magic which is indeed hard to convey. To understand it, one would have to imagine old Angelo Orsoni (d. 1969), the owner of a Venetian company of world renown, sitting in his blue boiler-suit by the window not far from his furnace, having a sample lump of molten glass paste brought to him and dipping it into a bucket of cold water before comparing it critically with the client's specimen; then, without using scales, carefully taking a spoonful of cobalt powder from a battered cocoa tin in order to deepen the ultramarine of the mixture and repeating the process until the required shade was matched precisely. Similarly, old Ugo Donà, founder of an equally renowned company on Murano, will point to a stack of smalto 'pancakes', one of the thousand or so in his store-room, saying, 'That translucent red there. . . . You know, I don't have to add anything to turn that into an opaque red – or even into a different colour.'

These leading factories, and two or three others in and around Venice, are family firms with only a handful of staff and, although they were established only a few decades ago, they are run in a spirit of almost medieval artisanship. Factories outside Italy, like Mittinger & Co. at Darmstadt in Germany, are rather more industrially organized. The layman will see little difference between Venetian smalti and those produced elsewhere, though the expert's eye notices the somewhat glassier and glossier appearance of non-Italian smalti and the mosaicist finds them brittler in cutting.

The basic ingredients of smalti are identical to those of ordinary glass: sand (silica), limestone (calcium carbonate), and alkalines (soda or potash) as a flux for reducing the melting point. The quality of the sand is important – Venice sends for it to Holland – and the percentage used in the mixture varies from 40% to 80%, depending on the properties required of the tesserae. To this basic glass compound are added opacifying agents, such as zinc oxide, cryolite, antimonic oxide, fluorite, arsenic oxide or red lead, in quantities determined by the desired degree of opacity; they also help to strengthen resistance to weather and breakage. Colour is obtained not by organic dyestuffs but by metal oxides, which are light-resistant. Various substances and quantities may be chosen, but typical formulae include:

red: selenium anhydride with cadmium sulphide. (Reds are the most expensive category.)
yellow: cadmium or uranium oxide
ochre: iron oxide or tin oxide
green: copper oxide or tin oxide
pale green: chromium oxide
pale blue: copper oxide
ultramarine: cobalt oxide
violet: cobalt oxide with cadmium oxide or selenium anhydride. (Because of the limited compatibility of these ingredients, violet shades are never entirely satisfactory – although this fact is hotly denied by some firms.)
black: high-percentage uranium salt
white: calcium carbonate and titanic oxide

For greater convenience in adjusting the colour of a mixture, Venetian companies keep 'master tints' – highly concentrated compounds in the form of smalti.

However, the chemical composition is not the whole story; the temperatures at which the mixture is fused in the furnace are also important, and these are determined by the colour required and the amount of sand in the mixture. They range from 1200° to 1500° Centigrade. The smelting process generally takes about twelve hours, after which lumps of the liquid mass are scooped on to a plate of metal (or, in earlier times, marble) and pressed to form circular discs appropriately called *pizze* ('pancakes'). Contact with the metal of the press leaves a light ripple on the surface, which adds life to it. Oxidation may cause a 'reaction', a crust a shade darker than the interior, which is not always desirable because what is eventually seen in the surface of the mosaic is normally the cut face of the tessera (i.e. part of the cross-section of the 'pancake'), so that, where a reaction occurs, each tessera will be framed by darkish outlines. The pancakes then travel for four to twelve hours on a conveyor belt through a (heated) cooling channel, where carefully graded reductions in temperature ensure the right consistency for breaking up into tesserae.

The mosaicist can use a pair of nippers to cut them in his studio as he wants them, but usually this is done by women in the factory. Strips are marked out by scratching lines on the surface of the disc which is then hacked into rectangular pieces, either by hammering over an upward-facing cutting edge, or with a hand-operated chopping machine. The most common size (*fig. 16*) is approximately 13 x 10 mm., but, since the cutting is done manually, there are variations and irregularities which contribute to the liveliness of the mosaic. Above all, the glitter of the tessera is due to the fact that the pancake is

Fig. 16 Cross-sections of tesserae:
1 Smalto tessera, surface about 13 x 10 mm. Two sides are smooth (originally top and bottom of the 'pancake'), all other surfaces fractured irregularly

2 Gold smalto tessera, smooth surface 20 x 20 mm. Made up of three strata: glass film on top, gold foil (white strip in diagram) and a base of ordinary glass

3 Vitreous tessera, smooth top surface 20 x 20 mm. The edges are bevelled (see text) and the bottom is rippled for better adhesion

143

not sawn evenly but chopped up, so that it splits un-evenly, according to stress conditions. This may cause an arch-like pattern to appear on the cut face, or it may reveal bubbles in the glass which will encourage the for-mation of a warm patina. The width of the tessera (i. e. the thickness of the original pancake) is normally 10 mm., in some cases 15 or 20 mm. There are also very thin pan-cakes, only 3 mm. in thickness, but these are used not as tesserae but as random shapes, with the pressed top sur-face (rather than the cut face) seen in the mosaic.

A special offshoot of mosaic, still practised as a sideline in the papal *Studio del Mosaico*, uses miniature tesserae of a type invented in the seventeenth or eighteenth cen-tury – *smalti filati*, or 'spun' smalti. The technique is based on smalti manufactured in the Vatican's own fac-tory from a particularly dense and intensely coloured substance containing crystal glass. Although the factory ceased to exist earlier this century, there are still supplies of its square tablets (rather than circular pancakes) with the papal mark imprinted on them. To make *smalti filati*, lumps of this material are melted over an open flame, drawn into strings resembling spaghetti and, when cold, clipped into pieces so small that they can barely be gripped between the fingers; their cut faces, being cross-sections of the spaghetti, are uniformly circular or oval. A mosaic composed of these tesserae, if not polished, has a peculiarly gritty texture which is quite in keeping with the medium. They seem, however, to have been a by-product of the desire to obtain very small tesserae with which to emulate the colour gradations of painting.

Another legacy of the endeavour to imitate painting is the almost incredible number of 28,000 shades of colour still stocked on the shelves of the Vatican workshop's 125ft-long store-room. As a rule, of course, mosaicists are quite content to have 300 to 1,000 in the studio. Leading factories keep selections of several thousand shades avail-able and, though the information they provide on the number of colours in stock may itself be a shade coloured, they will produce to order any tint an artist may fancy or a restorer may need to match the remaining tesserae in an ancient mosaic. Quite often, however, the difference between the various types of tessera is more one of con-sistency and texture than of colour. The so-called *mosaico antico*, for example, is obtained by mixing in extra sand at the end of the smelting process, so that it does not melt completely and its grains remain visible in the finished tesserae, lending them a sandstone-like character similar to those of ancient Ravenna.

Gold Mosaic

Gold mosaic is made with real gold. Some firms make about 200 different types of gold tesserae (one even claims to produce more than 500). As the material of the blazing

mural backgrounds, they have for fifteen centuries occu-pied a special place in the art of mosaic, as they do in smalti manufacture. While other smalti cubes are coloured throughout, gold smalti carry their golden glitter on the top side only – and it is this which forms the surface of the mosaic, not the cut face as in ordinary tesserae. They consist of three strata (*fig. 16*). The top one is pro-duced by blowing a sphere of very thin glass which, when cold, is cut into pieces of a manageable size. This glass film serves to protect the second stratum, 24-carat gold foil, which is then applied to it and heated for better adhesion. A thick layer of ordinary glass is now poured behind the first two, to act as a base and to make up the depth of normal tesserae. The material is finally cut into small squares or rectangles.

Here again, liveliness and warmth result from irregular-ities: from pores and veins, crinkles and cracks, thicker and thinner patches in the gold skin. Various angles of reflection are sometimes obtained within a single tessera by giving it a rippled surface. More commonly, differ-ences between the various types of gold tesserae are pro-duced either by tinting the thin top layer of glass or, more often still, by colouring the glass base underneath so that its colour will shine through the gold foil and modify its tone. A yellow base will intensify the gold's brilliance, a red base its richness, and in the same way a bluish or greenish sheen can be obtained which can decisively affect the general mood of the finished mosaic. There are also gold smalti with a tint so strong that they actually *are* blue, green or yellow, but have a type of brilliance different from that of ordinary, solidly-coloured smalti. In addition, there are silver and copper tesserae in which some manufacturers use silver and copper foil; the more fastidious Venetians, however, feel that these metals are unsatisfactory and always use gold, giving it a silver-white or copper-red tint.

All 'genuine' smalti are expensive, and in view of the immense number of varieties, the majority are produced in small quantities, frequently for an individual client only. Use of the more expensive ingredients is unavoid-able for the exact matching of certain shades. The cutting, on which so much of their individuality rests, is done by hand. For all these reasons Venetian smalti are sold at source (1970) for between 700 and 1300 lire per kilo-gram, depending on the colour, and golds for around 2000 lire. The average quantity required to cover one square foot is 1.5 kilograms. Cements and, especially, the labour involved in setting the irregular particles raise the price of finished mosaics to multiples of these amounts.

Vitreous Mosaic

Vitreous mosaic, which costs only about 200 lire per kilogram, is mostly applied as a straightforward wall-facing (in other words, as a building material), although it can also serve artistic purposes. There is some semantic confusion over the name, which is not entirely unjustified, because, as the adjective implies, vitreous mosaic is basically the same as glass mosaic. Just like 'genuine' smalti, it is sometimes referred to as 'Venetian' mosaic, which again can be factually correct, for some of the factories making it, though by no means all, are indeed situated around the Lagoon. However, the difference in quality between the two, although significant, is much smaller than the difference in price. What makes the production of vitreous mosaic more economic is concentration on a limited palette (only 80 colours are made by the leading Italian company, SAIVO) and avoidance of the more expensive raw materials. The dearest among vitreous tesserae are the smooth, so-called 'milky' ones with a relatively high content of fluorite as an opacifying agent. The more common type, however, is made of 'sanded' material, produced by the late addition of sand which is not melted completely – as in the *mosaico antico* among 'genuine' smalti. Sand not only makes vitreous mosaic cheaper, it also enlivens its even surface – and it is the smooth top surface of the 'pancake' which forms the reflective surface of the tessera, not the cut face, for vitreous 'pancakes' have a thickness of only 4 to 4.5 mm. Being so thin, vitreous mosaic offers the additional economic advantage that a kilogram covers a much larger area than in the case of the dearer smalti.

The manufacturing process is virtually identical to that of 'genuine' smalti – up to the stage when the glass compound is ready for the press. At this point a kind of waffle iron stamps a grid of grooves upon the thin vitreous pancake to prepare it for the machine which, after cooling, cuts it up into squares. The sloping sides of the squares now become bevelled edges of a tessera, which means that the back surface (which is to be embedded in plaster) is slightly smaller in area than the front (*fig. 16*). The most common format is 20 mm. (¾ in.) square, but there are also larger squares, rectangles, tesserae with rounded corners or with a curved surface to fit over the projecting angle between adjoining walls, as well as random pieces for crazy-paving effects. Another machine shakes the tesserae into the sunken squares of a small grid board, with narrow spaces between them to allow for grouting. The tesserae may be all of one colour, or different colours may be mixed, their exact positions in the grid being determined by chance. A sheet of paper is finally glued over the top. At the site, the paper is stripped off after the backs of the tesserae have been applied to the plastered wall: it is, in fact, a mechanized version of the indirect system of application. Another method is to glue the back surfaces of the tesserae to a coarse nylon net which remains buried in plaster when the joints are grouted. Apart from these ready-made facings, loose tesserae are, of course, available for individual artistic compositions.

Translucent Glass Mosaic

Small pieces of ordinary, non-opaque coloured glass are also used for mosaic decoration, normally being set on transparent bases and used for windows, lamps, vases, etc. A material specifically made for this purpose is the 'crystal glass mosaic' manufactured by the Austrian glass cutters D. Swarovski in minute tesserae starting from 2.5 mm. square, with a thickness of 1.5 mm.

Ceramic Mosaic

Clay, terracotta, bricks and tiles have always been used in mosaics, frequently in broken pieces or splinters and either by themselves or in conjunction with other materials. Specially made tesserae, not unlike the standardized *zalîj* tiles known in Islamic decoration, were frequently used for floors in the nineteenth century and have since gained even wider popularity for surfaces of all kinds. They are of two types: glazed and unglazed.

The unglazed material is coloured throughout and usually dull in appearance. The colouring substance is added in the beginning of the process, and the mixture is then dried, pressed and fired in temperatures ranging from 1100° to 1300° Centigrade, depending on colour and hardness. Glazed tiles, also known as 'faïence', have a white or buff body. The colour is only applied to the surface after firing and is fixed with the glazing process. Their somewhat cold lustre can be enlivened by slight mottling, and there is also a 'relief mosaic', with each tessera bearing furrows and ridges which produce changing light reflections.

In both types of ceramic mosaic, uses, formats and methods of application are similar to those of vitreous mosaic.

The Cartoon and Techniques of Transfer

A mosaic artist who takes his medium and his task seriously will start by examining the eventual site and considering its proportions, light conditions and the type and colour of the surrounding architectural elements – preferably in close contact with the architect. Having made some sketches, he paints, in colour, a 'cartoon' – not necessarily the full size of the mural, but laid out with due consideration for the structure of the mosaic-to-be: bold lines and areas, strong colour contrasts and (possibly) pointillistic colour mixtures, effective distribution of tonal values and of the various shapes and sizes of tesserae and a shape-giving deployment of their *andamento* (see below, Structure and Style). Nevertheless, the cartoon should not be excessively elaborate, with every tessera already marked, if the artist is not to lose that lively individuality which the tesserae only unfold in his hands during the actual setting.

This cartoon is kept by the artist's side as a model to work from, and rough outlines of the design may be marked on the working base. Such outlines are often found scratched in the cement under classical pavements and on medieval walls, where they are sometimes roughly sketched with a brush. Restoration work in S. Vitale in 1968–9 has even revealed, on the plaster underneath the mosaic, *sinopia* drawings which did not consist of outlines only but of fully painted colour areas – fresco paintings, in fact. This suggests that the artist, rather than pre-determining everything in his studio, worked out many points only on the wall itself, when he was able to see and judge the emerging mosaic literally 'in the light' of the building and could modify his plans accordingly – as occasional divergencies between the sketched outlines and the finished mosaic seem to imply.

There are several methods of transferring the design from the paper to the working base. Naturally, the cartoon will often be on a smaller scale than the intended mural, and both transfer and enlargement can be carried out in one operation by 'squaring up': i.e. covering both cartoon and working base with a proportionately scaled network of corresponding grid lines, and then copying the main features, square by square, from the cartoon on to the working surface. An alternative method is provided today by photographs and photographic enlargements. If working in the studio on a panel base, the photographic copy can be placed directly on this surface, or the artist may draw on the panel and the design may then be covered with wire-mesh to support the plaster, which is applied gradually as the mosaicist sets the tesserae in each successive patch. For other cases, where no enlargement is involved, there is the procedure practised in Ravenna today: a tracing is made of the principal lines which are then re-traced in ink on the reverse of the tracing paper. When this reverse side is laid on a carefully smoothed surface of moist lime, the ink lines will leave a perfect imprint. An analogous method consists in spreading graphite powder on the reverse of the tracing and then going over the lines with a hard pencil from the front side to leave an imprint on the working base as if using carbon-paper.

As the mosaicist takes tesserae from a series of boxes by his side, presses them into the plaster and establishes every delicate detail, his fingers are interpreting the cartoon in much the same way as a musical score is interpreted by the fingers on a keyboard.

Direct, Indirect and Reciprocal Setting

The *direct* system of setting tesserae simply means pressing them, face upward, into soft plaster. It is the most natural, the most expressive, in fact the classic system. It also permits full artistic use to be made of the differing angles of inclination (*fig. 15*, No. 6): the tesserae, applied with varying finger pressure, are not set absolutely parallel with the wall, but their surfaces (each in itself uneven) are turned this way or that, and their faceted multiplicity gives forth a vivid, ever-changing sparkle as the light's direction and the spectator's standpoint keep shifting. On the other hand, certain portions of a mural – perhaps a halo made of gold smalti, with their even surfaces – may radiate a more constant and concentrated brilliance if all its tesserae are uniformly inclined towards the strongest light, like flowers at a window (*fig. 15*, No. 5). The aesthetic advantage of a rough-set wall surface may, however, prove a disadvantage in practical terms, since it catches dirt and water more easily.

The *indirect* (or *reverse*) system produces a virtually plane surface almost automatically. Rather than being pressed into plaster, tesserae are first glued, face downward, on a paper or canvas sheet bearing the design – in lateral inversion, of course, for the image at this stage is seen from behind. This cartoon may also be cut into convenient sections (preferably coherent pictorial units, such as a head). When all the sections of the mosaic have been completed by this method, they are reassembled on the wall by pressing the reverse side into the plaster and the paper, which now covers the top surface, is soaked and stripped off like the paper on a child's transfer picture. Spare tesserae are set into cuts between the sections, which have initially been left ragged in order to facilitate closing them inconspicuously. Finally, the joints between tesserae are filled with grout.

The finished surface is as flat as the table with which the tessera have been in contact during setting, and the completed work has a colder look, more glaring but less sparkling, than a mosaic produced by the direct system – not only because it is a plane surface but also because the mosaicist has not been able to see the surface structure of the tesserae while applying them. By way of compensation, albeit a crude one, some mosaicists try afterwards to create a certain amount of diversity among the angles of the tesserae by hammering a board fitted with protruding nails against the surface while the mortar is still malleable. Nonetheless, the indirect system offers several important advantages. Work in the studio is more convenient as well as quicker, especially since a squad of mosaicists can work on their respective sections simultaneously. The design is easily and clearly drawn on the backing paper, and errors can be adjusted at any time because the tesserae are merely glued on. Above all, the sections on their thin backing are easily transportable.

The *reciprocal*, or *double reverse*, system (*mosaico a rivoltatura* or *su stucco provvisorio*) is more complicated than the other two but combines some of their respective advantages. It requires no tracing paper and no laterally reversed cartoon, and its use in classical times is therefore, theoretically, at least as conceivable as that of the indirect system; but all that can be said with certainty is that it was known by the end of the nineteenth century. Today there are several variants, depending on the material.

Strips of wood are used to frame a shallow bed of sand and lime, or of moist sand only. Outlines are sketched on this surface, and the tesserae are set as in the direct system. After the completed mosaic has dried, it is covered with flour paste or some other soluble adhesive in a coat thick enough to envelop the irregularities resulting from the varying angles, and several layers of gauze are spread on top and allowed to dry on. At this stage, the panel can be turned upside down, the original backing taken off and the sand-and-lime mixture removed completely from the back of the tesserae. This reverse side is now either applied to the wall, or else a permanent backing of plaster, concrete or polyester resin is poured over it, and, last of all, the gauze covering is stripped off the front, as in the indirect system.

Apart from the artistic advantages of varied tesserae angles and other subtleties of texture, there is the practical one that adjustments are feasible at several stages of the operation. With vitreous tesserae, too, this system avoids the necessity for a laterally reversed cartoon, the place of the temporary sand bed in this case being taken by a sheet of paper which bears the outlines of the design and to which the backs of the tesserae are glued.

Structure and Style
The various techniques of classical floor decoration are known to modern archaeology by the following terms:

opus signinum (p. 45): a mortar floor with fragments of stone or brick scattered at random (as in modern terrazzo) or arranged to form simple line patterns. An embryonic kind of mosaic.

opus segmentatum: a term used for similar floors reinforced with larger, random-shaped pieces of coloured limestone. Also applied to a crude type of *opus sectile*.

opus sectile (p. 8): coloured stones specially cut and neatly dovetailed; the shapes can be geometric (as in medieval Cosmati work) or figurative (resembling the 'Florentine mosaic' or *pietra dura* of a later age). This technique is related to inlay and must be distinguished from mosaic proper which has the anonymous tessera as its basic unit.

opus Alexandrinum, of (red) porphyry and (green) serpentine, may be regarded as a special type of *opus sectile*.

opus tessellatum (p. 46): tesserae of roughly equal rectangular shape and fairly coarse size (about 1 cm. square)

set in regular rows, which are normally straight but sometimes curved. Used particularly for neutral backgrounds or simple ornament.

opus reticulatum: an even more regular arrangement of squares set in both horizontal and vertical rows to form a grid system; it is found in classical wall construction, but not in Roman mosaic decoration (*pl. 95*).

opus vermiculatum (p. 46): small tesserae, occasionally only 1 sq. mm. and not necessarily rectangular, set in a 'wormlike' coursing which closely follows the shape of the design. Used particularly for intricate figurative work in the pictorial 'insert' or *emblema*.

opus musivum: a development of the Imperial period when the *emblema* was integrated with the rest of the mosaic and the distinction between *tessellatum* and *vermiculatum* dropped. The method of setting is determined by the character of each compositional element. As the tesserae are generally larger than in *vermiculatum*, their directional lines are more prominent.

The *andamento* – the 'coursing' or direction of the rows of tesserae and the interstices between them – is a characteristic means of expression in the mosaic idiom. Study of classical mosaics shows how it is used, in male figures particularly, for sharp delineation of muscles by *chiaroscuro*, whereas the soft curves of the female body may be rendered by gentle tonal gradations. Realistic differentiation of this kind gives way in the best murals of the Middle Ages to a more compact and concise stylization accompanied by even more wide-spread use of the *andamento*. It shapes and models, and, even in a uniformly white garment, can create the impression of drapery and depth.

Similar perspective effects are achieved by the tension between bright tones, which bring the object forward, and dark ones, which make it recede, but while this is equally true of painting, mosaic offers, in addition, the choice between larger tesserae, giving an impression of nearness, and smaller ones, giving an impression of distance. However, in a head, for example, the highlights of eyes, forehead and cheek-bones call for bright tones while at the same time their fine detail justifies small tesserae, which normally have a distancing effect; this cross-play between the functions of tonal and size values opens up a complex range of expressive permutations.

Intermediate colours can be rendered in mosaic without using tesserae of the intended shade: either according to strict divisionist theory by intermingling tesserae of primary colours so as to let them blend on the retina of the eye, or by doing the same with colours closer to the intended shade. While flat areas covered by tesserae of identical colour are, of course, possible, the technique of mingling is the logical application of the nature of a medium which is built up of fragments. For example,

147

skilful mosaicists, when interpreting a cartoon with a sky area indicated in plain blue, will not use a single colour throughout; they will start with a mixture containing seven or eight shades of tesserae, and will change over a few inches further on to a second, then a third and even more slightly different mixtures, in each of which the proportion of lighter blues is gradually increased – and the firmament will soar and will sparkle.

Restoration

Restoration today no longer means renovation in the taste of the restorer and of his time. Leaving some deplorable exceptions aside, a scholarly respect for the original prevails, materially helped by modern technology.

In order to enable missing tesserae to be accurately replaced, spares left over from other mosaics of the same period are collected and sorted. Where this source of authentic material fails, stones of matching colour and preferably of the same type of rock are prepared (cheaper substitutes may prove less durable), or smalti are specially made to match the pattern. Where a patch of tessellated pavement is irreparably lost, it is filled in with plain plaster so as to secure and support the remaining portion, and outlines may be painted on the plaster to suggest missing parts and give a more complete impression of the design. If, however, the floor is still to be walked on and gaps therefore have to be actually reconstructed, the new tesserae used to fill them should in honesty be seen to be new.

Where the base of the mosaic is crumbling, a total overhaul is necessary. Injections of liquid cement are now obsolete as they tend to endanger a mural by making it unduly heavy. The efficient rescue operation begins with meticulously photographing the old state and marking some points of reference by driving nails into the surface. Next, the decoration is broken up into coherent sections by removing a few tesserae along the cuts, the sections are numbered, and paper or gauze is glued to them (as in the reciprocal system of setting) before tools are inserted behind the mosaic to lift it off its base. On the table in the studio patient work with needles and small brushes removes any old mortar left on the back, and when it is clean, fresh cement is applied to re-fix it in its old place on the wall. The result is that all details, including the angles of the tesserae, remain authentic.

Analogous procedures are used to prepare both floor and wall mosaics for transport and for museum display. In the Carter workshop in London which does restoration work for the British Museum, epoxy resin, fibreglass and feather-light vermiculite granules (expanded mica) are applied in various layers, into which, as they are built up, strong bolts are inserted for fixing. The final backing is a neat plywood sheet.

The colours of classical stone pavements, which tend to look dull and dusty, revive brightly if a museum contrives to exhibit them under a shallow covering of water. A simpler way is to polish and at the same time protect them with wax or (better still) with that more durable product of modern chemistry: a coat of silicone.

Replicas

Replicas of mosaics can, of course, be made in the studio by translating good photographs back into tesserae, but much more fastidious procedures are practised in modern Ravenna. For mosaics with a plane surface, it is sufficient to take a tracing from the original, marking and colouring each tessera on the paper, and then transfer the outlines of all details to the working base (see above, The Cartoon and Techniques of Transfer). For rough-set murals, the mosaicist needs scaffolding so that he can climb up and press wet *papier-mâché* against the surface to obtain an impression which will record every tessera with its own particular angle, and the colour of each one is painted in watercolour in this negative mould. This, however, serves only as a model for reference, not as a mould for casting. Another way is to make a clay mould and produce a positive plaster cast from it, which is then coloured – but, again, this can only be used as a model. In either case, the actual replica is made by hand, tessera by tessera, following these models. A copy produced in this way is not a mechanical reproduction but a genuine mosaic based on an old mosaic.

Bibliography

Selection of books and papers used by the author

General
Edouard Gerspach, *La Mosaïque*, Paris n. d. [1881]
Adrien Blanchet, *La Mosaïque*, Paris 1928
Josef Ludwig Fischer, *Deutsches Mosaik und seine geschichtlichen Quellen*, Leipzig 1939
Edgar Waterman Anthony, *A History of Mosaics*, Boston 1935
Hans Unger, *Practical Mosaics*, London 1965
P. B. Hetherington, *Mosaics*, London 1967

Literary Sources
Vitruvius, *De architectura*, VII 1
Pliny the Elder, *Historia naturalis*, XXXV 110, XXXVI 184–9
Suetonius, *Divus Iulius*, 46
Moschion, quoted by Athenaeus in *Deipnosophistai*, V 207
Trebellius Pollio (one of the Scriptores Historiae Augustae), *Triginta Tyranni*, XXV 4
St Augustine, *De Civitate Dei*, XVI 8
Vasari, *Le vite*, chapters 6, 29, 30, 31

Antiquity
Julius Jordan, *1.–3. vorläufiger Bericht über die ... Ausgrabungen in Uruk-Warka*, (Abh. der Preussischen Akademie der Wissenschaften), Berlin 1930–2
Leonard Woolley *et al.*, *Ur Excavations: I Al-'Ubaid; II The Royal Cemetery*, London 1927 and 1934
F. Thureau-Dangin and Maurice Dunand, *Til-Barsib*, Paris 1936
— *Arslan-Tash*, Paris 1931
P. Gauckler, 'Musivum opus', in Daremberg-Saglio-Pottier, *Dictionnaire des antiquités grecques et romaines*, Paris 1904
Doro Levi, 'Mosaico', in *Enciclopedia dell'Arte Antica*, Rome 1963
H. P. L'Orange and P. J. Nordhagen, *Mosaics from Antiquity to the Early Middle Ages*, Oslo 1958, London 1966
Colloques Internationaux du Centre national de la recherche scientifique (1963), *La Mosaïque gréco-romaine*, Paris 1965
David M. Robinson (ed.), *Excavations at Olynthus: V, XII*, Baltimore and London 1933 and 1946
Marcel Bulard, *Peintures murales et mosaïques de Délos* (Monuments et mémoires de l'Académie des Inscriptions et de Belles Lettres, Fondation Eugène Piot, vol. 14), Paris 1908
Joseph Chamonard, *Les Mosaïques de la Maison des Masques* (Ecole Française d'Athènes, Exploration archéologique de Délos, fasc. XIV), Paris 1933
Joseph I. S. Whitaker, *Motya, A Phoenician Colony in Sicily*, London 1921
Georg Kawerau and Theodor Wiegand, *Die Paläste der Hochburg* (Altertümer von Pergamon, vol. 5), Berlin 1930

Albert Ippel, 'Mosaikstudien', in *Römische Mitteilungen* 45, Munich-Rome 1930, 80 ff.
Heinrich Fuhrmann, *Philoxenos von Eretria*, Göttingen 1931
Bernard Andreae, *Das Alexandermosaik*, Stuttgart 1967
Marion S. Blake, in *Memoirs of the American Academy in Rome*: 'The Pavements of the Roman Buildings of the Republic and Early Empire', VIII (1930), 7 ff; 'Roman Mosaics of the Second Century in Italy', XIII (1936), 67 ff.; 'Mosaics of the Late Empire in Rome and Vicinity', XVII (1940), 81 ff.
R. P. Hinks, *Catalogue of the Greek, Etruscan and Roman Paintings and Mosaics in the British Museum*, London 1933
Salvatore Aurigemma, *I mosaici di Zliten*, Rome-Milan 1926
Maria Floriani Squarciapino, *Leptis Magna*, Basle 1966
Giacomo Caputo and Abdelaziz Driss, *Tunisia: Ancient Mosaics*, UNESCO, Paris 1962
Abdelaziz Driss, *Trésors du Musée National du Bardo*, Tunis 1966
Biagio Pace, *I mosaici di Piazza Armerina*, Rome 1955
Gino Vincio Gentilini, *La Villa Imperiale di Piazza Armerina*, Rome n. d.
H. P. L'Orange, 'È un palazzo di Massimiano Erculeo che gli scavi di Piazza Armerina portano alla luce?', in *Simbolae Osloenses* XXIX (1952), 114 ff.
Jean Lassus, *Réflexions sur la technique de la mosaïque* (Les conférences-visites du Musée Stéphane Gsell), Algiers 1957
Klaus Parlasca, *Die römischen Mosaiken in Deutschland*, Berlin 1959
Doro Levi, *Antioch Mosaic Pavements*, 2 vols, Princeton-London-The Hague 1947
Günter Martiny, R. B. K. Stevenson and Gerard Brett, *The Great Palace of the Byzantine Emperors* (first report), London 1947
David Talbot Rice (ed.), *The Great Palace of the Byzantine Emperors* (second report), Edinburgh 1958
Meyer Schapiro and Michael Avi-Yonah, *Israel: Ancient Mosaics*. UNESCO, Paris 1960
Alfons M. Schneider, *The Church of the Multiplying of the Loaves and Fishes at Tabgha on the Lake of Gennesaret and its Mosaics*, Paderborn 1934, London 1937
Lluis Domenech i Montaner, *Centcelles. Baptisteri i celle-memoria de la primitiva esglesia-metropolitana de Tarragona*, Barcelona 1930
Helmut Schlunk, 'Untersuchungen im frühchristlichen Mausoleum von Centcelles', in *Neue deutsche Ausgrabungen im Mittelmeergebiet und im vorderen Orient* (Deutsches Archäologisches Institut), Berlin 1959, 344–65
Gian Carlo Menis, *I mosaici cristiani di Aquileia*, Udine 1965
Henri Stern, 'Les Mosaïques de l'église de Sainte-Constance à Rome', in *Dumbarton Oaks Papers* XII (1958), 157–218

Middle Ages

Augusto Agazzi, *Il mosaico in Italia*, Milan 1926

Walter Oakeshott, *The Mosaics of Rome from the third to the fourteenth centuries*, London 1967

Guglielmo Matthiae, *Mosaici Medioevali delle chiese di Roma*, Rome 1967

Giuseppe Bovini, *Ravenna Mosaics*, Milan-Greenwich, Conn. 1956, London 1958

— *Ravenna – Città d'Arte*, Ravenna 1956

David Talbot Rice, *Byzantine Art* (rev. ed.), London 1968

— and Max Hirmer, *The Art of Byzantium*, London 1959

André Grabar, *Byzantine Painting*, Geneva 1953

— and M. Chatzidakis, *Greece: Byzantine Mosaics*, UNESCO, Paris 1959

— *Greek Mosaics of the Byzantine Period*, UNESCO, London 1964

Otto Demus, *Byzantine Mosaic Decoration*, London 1948

— *The Mosaics of Norman Sicily*, London 1949/50

— *The Church of San Marco in Venice*, (Dumbarton Oaks Studies), Cambridge, Mass. 1960

— 'Studies among the Torcello mosaics', in *The Burlington Magazine*, 83–4 (1943–4)

V. N. Lazarev, *Old Russian Murals and Mosaics*, London 1966

— *Mozaiki Sofii Kievskoy*, Moscow 1960

Olexa Powstenko, *The Cathedral of St Sophia in Kiev*, New York 1954

K. A. C. Creswell, *Early Muslim Architecture*, 2 vols, Oxford 1932, 1940

Marguerite van Berchem, 'The Mosaics of the Dome of the Rock in Jerusalem and of the Great Mosque at Damascus', in Creswell, *op. cit.* vol. I

Ernst Kitzinger, *Israeli Mosaics of the Byzantine Period*, UNESCO, London 1965

Percy Brown, *Indian Architecture* (2 vols), 5th ed., Bombay 1965, 1968

Edmund W. Smith, *Moghul Colour Decoration*, (Archaeological Survey of India, vol. 30), Allahabad 1901

Marshall H. Saville, *Turquois Mosaic Art in Ancient Mexico* (Museum of the American Indian, Haye Foundation), New York 1922

Modern period

James Johnson Sweeney and Josep Lluís Sert, *Antoni Gaudí*, London 1960

E. Casanelles, *Antonio Gaudi. A Reappraisal*, Barcelona 1965, London 1967

Gino Severini, 'Mosaico e arte murale nell'antiquità e nei tempi moderni', in *Felix Ravenna* LX (1952), 21–37

Leonardo Ricci, 'Il mosaico vetroso e la sua problematica', in *Civiltà delle Macchine* (SAIVO house magazine), September-October 1958

Fritz R. Barran, *Kunst am Bau – heute*, Stuttgart 1964

Paul F. Damaz, *Art in European Architecture*, New York 1956

— *Art in Latin American Architecture*, New York 1963

Jeanne Reynal, *et al.*, *The Mosaics of Jeanne Reynal*, New York 1964

Joseph L. Young, *Mosaics: Principles and Practice*, New York 1963

Rokuro Yabashi, *Mosaic*, Tokyo 1970

Technique

Isotta Fiorentina Roncuzzi, *Tecnologia del mosaico*, Ravenna 1964

Louisa Jenkins and Barbara Mills, *The Art of Making Mosaics*, Princeton 1957

Mary Lou Stribling, *Mosaic Techniques*, London-New York 1966

Helen Hutton, *Mosaic Making*, London-New York 1966

John Berry, *Making Mosaics*, London 1966

Acknowledgments

The reproductions were made with the kind permission of the museums, collections and authorities named in the captions. Material for reproduction was kindly supplied by the following: Alinari, Florence: *Pls 10–12, 17, 19–23, 26, 44, 60–1, 77*; Anderson, Rome: *Pls 7–8, 25, 27, 57, 66–71*; Georg Baur, Hamburg: *Pl 84*; Fane C. Braham: line drawing, p. 141; British Museum, London: *Pls 1–2, 74, 79*; Hillel Burger, Jerusalem: *Pls 89–90*; Deutsches Archäologisches Institut, (Madrid): *Pls 36, 72*; (Rome): *Pl. 29*; Klaus Eid, Mexico: *Pls XV, 96–8, 102–3*; Photo-Emka Ltd, Jerusalem: *Pls 40, 75*; Heinz Finke, Konstanz: *Pl. 91*; Foto E. P. T., Ravenna: *Pl. 43*; Foto Gnilka, Berlin: *Pl. 86*; Giraudon, Paris: *Pl. 13*; Hatay Museum, Antakya: *Pls 30–2*; Hans Hinz, Basle: *Pls IX–X*; Hirmer-Fotoarchiv, Munich: *Pls 50, 55, 78*; Nicos Kontos, Athens: *Pl. 6*; Kurt Lackner, Vienna: *Pl. XI*; A. Longo, Ravenna: *Pl. 46*; Franz Mayer'sche Hofkunstanstalt, Munich: *Pl. 85*; Heinz Müller-Brunke, Grassau, Bavaria: *Pl. 63*; Musée Fernand Leger, Biot: *Pl. XII*; Musée National du Bardo, Tunis: *Pls 28, 37*; Propyläen-Verlag, Berlin: *Pls 5–18;* Jochen Remmer, Munich: *Pls 53, 59, 64*; Rheinisches Bildarchiv, Cologne: *Pls 14–15*; David Talbot Rice, Edinburgh: *Pl. 33*; E. Richter, Rome: *Pl. 24*; Foto Ritter, Vienna: *Pl. 80*; John A. Rose, Kenton, Harrow: *Pl. 99*; Scala, Milan: *Pls I–V, VII*; John D. Schiff, New York: *Pl. 104*; Herbert Schwingenschlögl, Vienna: *Pl. 88*; Photoatelier Norbert Segal, Tel Aviv: *Pl. XIV*; Staatliche Landesbildstelle Saarland, Saarbrücken: *Pl. 16*; Staatliche Museen, Berlin: *Pls 3, 9*; Foto Umberto Trapani, Ravenna: *Pl. 81*; Mario Tschabold, Steffisburg: *Pl. XIII*; Fototeca Unione, Rome: *Pl. 35*; Verlagsarchiv Schroll: *Pls 4, 34, 42, 58, 62, 65, 73, 76*; A Villani & Figli, Bologna: *Pls 45, 47*; August Wagner, Berlin: *Pls 82–3*; Charles Wehner, London: *Pl. XVI*.

The author wishes to record his gratitude to the many artists, scholars, museum officials and companies who have given advice and assistance, and regrets that he is able to single out only the young librarians of the Victoria and Albert Museum in London whose untiring helpfulness has opened so many doors to information.

Index